WALKING
WITH THE NIGHT

WALKING
WITH THE NIGHT

THE AFRO-CUBAN
WORLD OF SANTERIA

RAUL CANIZARES

DESTINY BOOKS
ROCHESTER, VERMONT

Destiny Books
One Park Street
Rochester, Vermont 05767

Note to the reader: This book is intended as an informational guide. The remedies, approaches, and techniques described herein are given for illustrative purposes only. Neither the author nor the publisher recommends their use.

LIBRARY OF CONGRESS CATALOGING-IN-PUBLICATION DATA

Canizares, Raul, 1955-
    Walking with the night : the Afro-Cuban world of Santeria / Raul Canizares.
      p.   cm.
    Includes bibliographical references and index.
    ISBN 0-89281-366-0
    1. Santeria (Cultus)   I. Title.
BL2532.S3C37 1992
299'.67—dc20   92-4941
                                       CIP

Printed and bound in the United States

10 9 8 7 6 5 4 3 2 1

Destiny Books is a division of Inner Traditions International, Ltd.

Distributed to the book trade in the United States by American International Distribution Corporation (AIDC)

Distributed to the book trade in Canada by Book Center, Inc., Montreal, Quebec

Text design by Randi Jinkins

Cover painting: *Eleggua*, by Cuqui Aponte, oil on canvas, 50" x 54"

To Father Pat Moloney

Note on names: Full names appearing here (Paco Cuevas, German Perez) are the actual names of people. Single names or initials (Ifá P., Balu) are pseudonyms.

Note on orthography: The traditional Cuban hispanicized spelling of Lucumí words is used throughout. No effort has been made to render them into standard Yoruba. Yoruba speakers, however, will have no trouble recognizing in the Lucumí *babalao* the Yoruba *baba l'awo,* in the Lucumí *Oshún* the Yoruba *osun,* and so on.

CONTENTS

ACKNOWLEDGMENTS

A considerable amount of information contained in this work was the direct result of research undertaken by me in order to complete my master's thesis in Religious Studies at the University of South Florida. I would like to express my thanks to my thesis committee, composed of Michael Angrosino, Mozella Mitchell, Joseph Murphy, and Nathan Katz. I am also enormously indebted to William Shea, who selflessly helped me shape the ideas that have gone into this book. There is more of Professor Shea in this work than even he suspects. To my pal Jill Lones, all-knowing secretary of the University of South Florida's Religious Studies department, I owe a lot of encouragement and good will.

I am deeply indebted to Dr. William Heim, University of South Florida Religious Studies and English professor recognized as an authority in so-called occult religions, who so graciously wrote a foreword to this work, and to Omi Dina, whose perspective enlightened my understanding of how non-Cubans view Santeria. I am also indebted to Ade Atare, who first suggested I send Inner Traditions the manuscript of *Walking with the Night*. Other scholars who have helped me gain a greater understanding of not just the issues discussed in this book but of religion in general, include Darrell

Fasching, James Strange, and Jacob Neusner, all of the University of South Florida. Heartfelt thanks also go to the staff of the University of South Florida's Inter-Library Loan Department, especially Sharon Epps and Mary Kay Hartung, who diligently helped me obtain rare Santeria manuscripts and articles. I also want to thank Professor Andres Isidoro Perez y Mena of Rutgers University, whose insights helped me develop the Santeria cosmogony diagram included in this work (Figure 2). To thank those in the Santeria community, both living and dead, who have contributed to my understanding of the religion would be redundant, for this is their book as much as it is mine.

At Inner Traditions I have found outstanding support and encouragement from editor in chief Leslie Colket as well as from publisher Ehud Sperling. Art director Estella Arias's contributions to the book are invaluable. Thanks also to Lee Wood and all the other professionals at Inner Traditions who have made such positive contributions to *Walking with the Night.* Copy editor Cornelia Bland Wright did an outstanding job of turning a jumbled maze of potentially interesting stories into a cohesive whole; for this I thank her.

Finally, my deepest thanks and most heartfelt gratitude is reserved for the brilliant Religious Studies scholar Nathan Katz, who as my mentor for a number of years has believed in me and in my work and has offered me incredible support. Professor Katz encouraged me to systematically research Santeria and gave me the tools to do so in a scholarly manner. The word "thanks" is highly inadequate to express my debt to Dr. Katz, but it will have to do.

FOREWORD

Santeria, a religion of beauty and resilience, is often erroneously classified as "primitive" in relation to the monotheistic faiths of the West. This notion is misguided. Santeria is most certainly not the primitive religion of a backward people. In the pages that follow, Raul Canizares demonstrates that Santeria is the thoughtful and deliberate response of a thinking people to a hostile social environment. It is the faith of a people experiencing their own diaspora and, at its roots, is as true to its origins as modern Judaism is to the days when the Temple stood.

The general impression of Santeria as a polytheistic religion does not stand close scrutiny. Just as the saints of the Catholic Church serve as patrons to various human concerns without detracting from the oneness of God, so the orishas, depicted in the guises of saints, are the projections of a single, primal force: ashé. This force evolved into awareness—Olodumare—and then into action—Olofi. Through Olofi ashé was made manifest in the generations of orishas, who represent specific aspects of the force in ways more or less comprehensible to mortals. I am reminded of the Kabbalistic mysteries of Western tradition: the primal state of being, *ain,* evolved into awareness through the veils of negative existence, *ain soph* and *ain soph aur,* to achieve manifestation through the ten emanations that result in the created universe. Here, each of the ten aspects of the divine mind is comprehended, through personifications, as an archangel. With knowledge of the correspondences between celestial forces and the mundane, the adept can effect change on the physical plane and personal growth on the spiritual.

I am not suggesting that Santeria and the Hermetic Kabbalah have more similarities than differences. I do suggest, however, that those who approach the study of Santeria expecting to find a primitive religion should look to their own houses and discard an adjective that is meaningless. If Santeria is primitive, then we all share the same cave.

This is a needed book, especially since Santeria is on the brink of becoming a world religion. The author combines the training of a scholar and a lifetime of experience to create a work both objective and sympathetic. Scholarship and personal narrative are masterfully blended here in what may prove to be the finest study of Santeria to appear in English.

I invite you, then, to accompany Raul Canizares on a brief walk with the night. You may glimpse vague shadows and hear strange drums, but in the end there was really nothing to fear, and your map can only be more useful for adding one more path.

William J. Heim
Professor of English and affiliate of
the Department of Religious Studies
University of South Florida

INTRODUCTION

Acting on a tip, a raiding party of police officers and agents of an animal protection society went to a tenement in the Bronx yesterday afternoon and interrupted a *primitive* religious rite involving the ritual slaughter of animals . . . the people in the apartment acknowledged they were followers of a cult known as Santeria . . . *[which] once practiced infanticide as well as animal sacrifices. . . .*[1]

This sensationalist statement did not appear in a supermarket tabloid but in the respected *New York Times.* Misinformation about Santeria in the media appears to be the norm rather than the exception. At times, reports of a purportedly academic nature are no better. The reasons why traditions such as those of Africa, India, aboriginal Australia, and the native peoples of North and South America are open to experiences that are not part of the sensorium of most Western peoples may lie in the values such societies hold dear. Unused concepts, like muscles, tend to lose their efficacy; figuratively speaking, people in Western societies have not made use of the "muscles" involved in seeing beyond the immediately tangible or the material for so long that they have forgotten how to do so. Fortunately, in the midst of incredulity and doctrinaire beliefs, there are people intensely interested in finding out if there is something of value in the ancient traditions of non-Western societies. These seekers are usually rewarded with an expanded consciousness that enriches their lives.

What is Santeria? It is neither a re-created religion, such as Wicca, nor a new religion. Santeria's roots go back uninterruptedly at least as far as any other of the living ancient faiths. The religion we now refer to as Santeria began, like all life, in Africa. Specifically it began in the Nile Valley, among a people called the Twa. From the original Twa grouping, four major branches developed and traveled away from the center; those to the north became known as Ta-Merrians or Aegyptians, those to the south as Amazulus, those to the east as Agikuyus, and those to the west as Yorubas.[2] Forty thousand years ago, the Twa conceived of God in a way that became the basis of many African religions. The Twa called their God simply Greatest Creator of All—The Unknown. The Ta-Merrians called this God Aten, while the Yorubas called him Olodumare.

Yoruba civilization goes back at least a thousand years to the founding of Ile-Ife, holy city of the Yoruba and center of their empire. Yoruba scholars have advanced diverse ideas as to the origin of the Yoruba, some even suggesting a relationship to Middle Eastern countries. The staff of Oranyan, a monolith said to be a thousand years old that is a symbol of the Yoruba, has the Hebrew letter *yod* carved near its pinnacle.

When European merchants, dealers in human suffering, arrived at the shores of West Africa in the sixteenth century, the magnificence of Yoruba culture had already begun to wane. However, exquisite works of art, especially in sculpture, attest to the greatness of the civilization that spread from Ife to a great part of Western Africa. The Yoruba achieved legendary status not only in art but also in religion. The beauty of Yoruba religious myths rivals those of ancient Greece.

The disintegration of the Yoruba empire can be traced to the fall of Alafin Awole in 1796. Muslim invasions by Fulani tribesmen in the early part of the nineteenth century resulted in hundreds of thousands of Yorubas finding themselves in chains, many losing their lives and being shipped to the New World as slaves in the infamous Middle Passage.

Among the Yorubas, Olodumare—also called Olorun—was the greatest of all divinities, the one who parceled out portions of ashé, the source of all power, among the lesser divinities, called orishas. The High God Olodumare was thought of as being too far removed from humankind to help with everyday problems; for this the Yorubas and their New World descendants, the Lucumí and the Nagos, turned to the orishas.

The main area of Yorubaland lies in the southwestern part of the modern nation of Nigeria, though considerable numbers of Yorubas live in the neighboring countries of Benin and Ghana. During the dark and shameful days of the slave trade, hundreds of thousands of Yorubas were taken from their homeland and sold as chattels in North, Central, and South America, as well as in the Caribbean. In certain parts of the New World, for reasons we will examine later, the Yoruba people were able to preserve important elements of their faith. They were particularly successful in preserving their culture in Cuba, where they became known as Lucumís, and in Brazil, where they became known as Nagos. The term Yoruba originally referred only to the people of the city-state of Oyo; it first was used to refer to all other members of the Ife hegemony in the nineteenth century.

The city of Ife, called Ile-Ife, is thought in Yoruba belief to be the cradle of creation. The paramount chief of Ife, called the Oni of Ife, is thought of as the spiritual ruler of all the Yorubas. As Yoruba religion underwent the necessary adaptations in order to survive in the hostile Cuban environment, eventually becoming known as Santeria, its devotees continued to revere Ife. For example, the slaves would sing this song as they worked: "While my body in Cuba wilts, my soul in Ife blooms." Over time, Ife became an abstract, almost subliminal memory.

It was in song that much of the power of Yoruba religion was preserved. Drumming and singing required just three components—

a voice, two hands, and a hard surface—yet this deceptively simple trio of components harbored enormous supernatural power. The Spanish authorities in Cuba tolerated the use of drumming and singing by the slaves without realizing that what the slaves were doing was not entertainment but an extremely powerful religious ritual. Had the Catholic authorities suspected the religious function of the slaves' music, they would have forbidden its use and Santeria would never have developed in Cuba.

Part of the appeal of Santeria is certainly its sensuality. Santeria is what can be described as an embodied religion, one that is felt with the entire body, that in turn feeds the soul. The rhythmic patterns of Santeria drumming are said to cause sympathetic re-actions in the human body—at least in the bodies of believers—ranging from sedation to arousal, depending on the song. The immediacy of the divine, so accessible to santeros, is attractive to those raised in traditions that tend to view God as inaccessible. Just as African spirit revolutionized American culture through jazz, rock and roll, rhythm and blues, and Afro-Cuban music, it is now making an impact on religious practices.

While it began as the religion of slaves, Santeria is now practiced by people from all walks of life. It is practiced by Western people, yet it is not a Western religion. This paradox has contributed to much of the confusion surrounding the question of Santeria's morality. Santeria's value system cannot be objectively characterized as being either superior or inferior to that of Western Christianity. What can be asserted is that the worldview of Santeria differs from that of the Judeo-Christian and Islamic faiths; therefore, the ethical framework found in Santeria is correspondingly different from that found in Western religions.

> In the beginning was Ashé. When Ashé began to think, Ashé became Olodumare. When Olodumare acted, He became Olofi, and it was Olofi who out of a part of himself created Obatalá.

The concept of ashé is central to understanding right and wrong in Santeria. Ashé—from the Yoruba *Asé*—is, like the Hindu term *dharma*, a dynamic and hard-to-define concept. While the word *ashé* has become part of the popular Cuban lexicon, meaning "luck" or "charisma," its ontological meaning is much deeper, referring to a sense of order and balance in the universe. Ashé is the ultimate source of everything.

Santeros, or priests of Santeria, view the universe—including God and the orishas—as being inhabited by codependent beings who have responsibilities to one another. These responsibilities, spelled out in such orally transmitted works as the oracle of Ifá, are all conducive to the attainment of order and balance. Imbalance (lack of ashé) is experienced by the individual as a dysfunctional emotional, physical, or economic state. When a person experiences imbalance, he or she consults one of the oracles of Santeria to find out the cause of the imbalance and an appropriate remedy. This usually involves some sort of offering to the orishas or to ancestral spirits, as well as practical advice from the reader of the oracle—usually a santero or santera—on how to regain the lost balance.

Western bipolarities such as good and evil or God and Satan have little meaning in Santeria.[3] For santeros, "evil" is a relative term; there are no absolutes. Evil, sin, and pain can all be defined as lack of ashé—imbalance. A "good" person by Western standards could conceivably fit Santeria's definition of evil as one who causes imbalance. The following hypothetical case will demonstrate what I mean:

> A Roman Catholic priest in a small Latin American town cuts down a tree to which local santeros give offerings. The priest feels he is helping his neighbors by eliminating a temptation to practice idolatry, a mortal sin. The santeros, however, feel that the Catholic priest has caused a very serious imbalance. One santero consults an oracle, which indicates that the Catholic priest will suffer the consequences of having caused this imbalance. That night, the priest suffers a heart attack and dies. Christians denounce the santeros as belonging to a satanic cult that used black magic to harm a saintly man.

From the Christian perspective, the Catholic priest could be defended for following the dictates of his faith. From the santeros' perspective, however, the priest cut down a sacred entity and a repository of ashé; he thus committed an act of unprovoked aggression tantamount to murder. Santeros would view the priest's death as indicative of his culpability. An argument from a Santeria perspective would be that the hypothetical priest's problem was the faulty value system to which he subscribed—the "thou shalt nots" of the Judeo-Christian tradition. The rigid ethics of Western Christianity, a santero might argue, consist of an arbitrary set of rules imposed from the outside, rules that, because of their static nature, are irrelevant to specific situations. Santeros believe that a more realistic, naturalistic, and, yes, moral course of action is the one that is dictated by a person's own ashé. Santeros believe that each person's ashé internally inspires him or her to act harmoniously, in a manner congruent with the avoidance of imbalance. Imbalance is caused when a person has difficulty accessing his or her ashé. When they experience difficulties, believers try to learn how to regain access to their ashé. In these situations specialists such as babalaos are employed. Many times, a babalao, or member of the highest order of priest in Santeria, will contact a person's eledá—personal orisha, or "guardian angel"—to ask him or her for help in restoring balance to the afflicted person.

Although my background, Spanish-Yoruba-French-Italian-Canary Islander-Filipino-Native American, may seem complex by U.S. standards, it is not uncommon for Cubans to exhibit such mixed ancestries (Cuba is, in my opinion, much more of a "melting pot" than the United States ever was). My mother, a Santeria priestess, came from a long line of Yoruba priests and priestesses who traced their roots back to the city of Oyo in Africa. My first initiation occurred before I was born, a dedication ceremony in which I was preordained to be a priest of Obatalá, chief of all orishas. By the time I was seven years old I had already received most of the initiations a santero can receive, including the all-important kariocha (literally, "to be seated in the head" in Lucumí) initiation. In this ceremony, one's ruling orisha is ritually embedded in one's head through a process that includes shaving the head and cutting a small wound in the scalp where the secrets of the orisha—in the form of a pastelike substance made secretly by the initiating priests and priestesses—are placed. When the wound heals, the orisha's ashé (grace, power) becomes forever a part of the santero's being.

As a scholar, I have dedicated myself to the serious academic study of Santeria. I hold a master's degree in religious studies from the University of South Florida and am presently working on my doctoral dissertation in anthropology. The fact that I know the inner workings of this powerful religion intimately and also possess the academic tools to interpret it credibly places me in a unique position. By utilizing this combination I hope to bring some needed cohesion to Santeria studies, a discipline that is gaining importance due to the increasing number of people—of all ethnic backgrounds—who are choosing to become part of the tradition.

Although my formal research has focused on the degree of deliberateness with which Santeria practitioners made use of Catholic disguises in order to preserve their faith in a hostile environment, I find that this information makes more sense when presented as a component of a larger theoretical framework. In this book, I present the deception/dissimulation factor alongside other important components of Santeria, especially the hierarchical stages of the religion.

Because of my personal history with Santeria, an important part of this book is the anecdotal narratives it contains; they illustrate aspects of Santeria that in any other form would be difficult for outsiders to grasp. The nature of these narratives defies the boundaries of everyday reality, yet I can honestly say that in this book I am exercising great restraint in not including material that in Western societies would be deemed truly unbelievable. As much as I can, I have restricted myself to presenting this work in an academically defensible fashion. There may come a time in the future, however, when it will be appropriate to fully discuss the myriad supernatural events I, as well as many others involved in non-Western traditions, have experienced.

Finally, this book will complement other fine scholarly works on Santeria by offering the unique perspective of a scholar who was born into the tradition. After a careful review of the literature and of present scholarship on Santeria, I've reached the conclusion that the perspective of the high-level initiate—the priests and priestesses, as well as the high priests of the religion—has not been adequately portrayed and is not accessible to the English-speaking community. As one born into the tradition, I possess unique tools to aid my scholarly research. This union of experience with academic discipline—of the -emic with the -etic—will serve us well in exploring hitherto unchartered aspects of the fascinating religion of Santeria.

Although I have not practiced Santeria as my personal religion for a number of years, I continue to hold the religion in very high esteem. I always advise my informants that I no longer consider myself an insider, but because of my previous involvement with and familial ties to the religion, neither am I considered an outsider. For the most part, my numerous informants have been very understanding and supportive of the work of this outsider-insider. Their sole wish, that I do not reveal the particulars of my own initiations, will be honored. For the purposes of accurate scholarship, however, I will refer to published accounts of initiations that I consider accurately written.

---NOTES---

1. Robert McFadden, "Ritual Slaughter Halted in Bronx by Police Raid," *New York Times*, May 24, 1980, sec. 27, p1.
2. Josef Ben-Jochannan, "Another Dimension to Zulu Christianity," in *The Long Search* (Dubuque, Iowa: Kendall-Hunt Publishing, 1978), 56-57.
3. In modern Yoruba thought, bipolarities are becoming increasingly evident because of Judeo-Christian and Islamic influences.

CHAPTER 1

—

MANTILLA

"But Padrino," said the scared little boy, "I cannot go out there alone, I am afraid of the dark, I am afraid of the night."

"You must not fear the dark, for the dark is the womb from where all life springs; neither must you fear the Night, for the Night is your friend, the bringer of rest," said the old babalao. "Learn to walk with the Night and she will be a good companion."

Confused by the old man's peculiar use of language, the little boy asked, "You mean walk at night, or through the night?"

"No, my son, walk with it—never through it or in it."

It would be a long time before that little boy understood the significance of the high priest's words that dark and magical night. As part of a pre-kariocha initiation, the boy was required to commune with the spirits of the forest by spending a night alone in a sacred grove not far from the padrino's house. The old man was trying to instill in his young charge a respect for nature. Santeros do not personalize aspects of nature because they are ignorant or naive: they do so as a way of emphasizing the inter-relatedness of all things. The little boy met his padrino again several days later, in a place called Mantilla.

Not much seemed different, that Saturday evening long ago, as my mother and I prepared to go out. From the terrace of our eleventh-floor condominium overlooking Havana Harbor, we could see the overcast sky. My father, a prominent physician, was at one of his medical conventions; the regular chauffeur, Ramon, had gone with him. Andres, a serious-looking bearded mulatto[1] who filled in for Ramon occasionally, stood solemnly in the hallway waiting for the lady of the house. "The car is ready, señora," said Andres. Within minutes, my mother's 1957 Buick Special emerged from the under-ground garage. Our destination was not one of Havana's fashionable shops or the lakeside park we often visited on Saturday afternoons. Mother, Andres, and I were heading toward the outskirts of Havana to a place called Mantilla. The geographical distance between our neighborhood and Mantilla was not significant. However, the reli-gious, social, and racial differences between the white enclave of wealth and aristocracy known as El Vedado—the forbidden zone— and the predominantly black, desperately poor township of Mantilla could not have been greater. As the big, black Buick left behind the sterile paved boulevards of El Vedado and entered the blood-red mud pathways of Mantilla, a change came over its three occupants. No longer was Andres the part-time chauffeur taking his rich employer and her little boy out for a drive; he became an elder santero who was guiding his young sister in religion and her son

to a world of pulsating rhythms and magic, a world as far removed
from El Vedado as Lagos is from Madrid.

It had been raining hard that day and Mantilla's red clay roads
had the consistency of porridge. Andres finally stopped the car and
said we had to continue on foot for the last 150 feet to Amanda's
compound, visible in a clearing in the middle of the bush. Dusk was
setting in and the sky was as red as the soil. Andres took this to
mean that Shangó, the orisha of lightning, was going to make his
royal presence felt that night (Shangó's emblematic color is red).

Amanda was a santera, or priestess, whose bembé we would take
part in (a bembé is a feast given by a santero or santera in honor
of an orisha, usually in thanksgiving or to repay a favor the orisha
has conferred). Her compound consisted of a large, rectangular
wooden building with a corrugated-iron roof and four smaller thatched
structures, two on each side of the bigger one. The five houses
formed a semicircle around a four-foot-high, dome-shaped shrine
of coral rock. This was the home of Amanda's Eleggua, the orisha
who guards the doorways and is lord of the pathways. From his
central position, Eleggua watched over Amanda's ilé (household).

Apparently Amanda was not the only santera offering a bembé
to the orishas that night in Mantilla, for as we approached the big
house the incessant drumming and chanting of several feasts reached
our ears from all four cardinal points. A chorus of bullfrogs offered
a primal counterpoint to the chanting and the drumming, creating
a preternatural symphony of overpowering beauty. As we entered
the large living room, we noticed about twenty-five people, mostly
black women, merrily chatting, laughing, and mingling. It was a
typical party scene except for two things: nearly everyone was
dressed in white, and no one was eating or drinking—that would
come later.

The women were wearing long, flowing skirts and white scarves
on their heads. Most wore multicolored beaded necklaces that identified them as believers in Santeria. Andres' dark business suit and
tie and my mother's black evening dress and silver fox stole looked
curiously out of place. Both of them were obviously well known,

however, for they were warmly greeted by those around them. A very small, light-skinned black woman, apparently in her seventies, made her way through the crowd. She was Zena, Andres' mother, one of Amanda's principal helpers. Zena was a renowned Santeria dancer; even at her advanced age, she was able to perform the orishas' ancient, complicated steps from sunset to daybreak. After exchanging greetings with Andres, Zena invited my mother to freshen up at her place before she took her to see Amanda. Zena and Andres occupied the two-room hut just west of the main house. One of Amanda's rich clients had recently had a modern bathroom and running water installed in the main house, but the other houses in the compound did not yet possess such amenities.

Hiding her platinum hair under a white scarf and wearing the long, flowing skirt Zena had given her, Roxana looked quite different from the white lady she seemed to be a few minutes before. It was as if her African heritage, hidden under her father's European skin, had emerged from some recondite spot within her where it had lain dormant, waiting to be called. Andres, Mother, and I reentered the big house through a back room where five men sat on straw mats quietly talking among themselves. They were wearing the green and yellow beaded sashes that identified them as babalaos, the high priests of Santeria. One of the men was Juan García, our padrino. Mother and I prostrated ourselves in front of the old man, chanting "Iború iboyaibó cheché," the ancient salute to the babalaos (even Africans say this is untranslatable, but it may refer to the three women associated with the mythic first babalao). Padrino stood, helped Mother up, and warmly embraced her in the traditional Santeria way by bumping shoulders, left to left, right to right.

Sitting on a goatskin stool known as a *taburete,* off to one side of the room, Amanda was apparently deep in thought. As we approached her, Amanda stood to her full six feet. She was a slender woman of regal bearing whose unlined, open face and huge brown eyes belied her sixty-two years. Amanda had beautiful, unblemished skin the color of copper; her smile revealed a set of perfect white teeth. Before Mother could prostrate herself in front of Amanda in the traditional *moforibale* salute, Amanda embraced her and kissed her on the cheek.

"I'm glad the big movie star found time to come see her old Madrina," joked Amanda.

"Papa Shangó would not have it any other way," replied Mother, who was a daughter (devotee) of Shangó. My mother told me, "Madrina was the one who predicted that Obatalá would give me a son born on his feast day who would bear his mark;[2] that was you."

"I wasn't the one who predicted it, Roxana," countered Amanda, "don't you remember I was *montada* [possessed] that day? Obatalá himself told you that prophecy!"

"Andres!" continued Amanda. "Tell the girls to start serving, I think people are getting hungry. Oh, and tell them the good news that Obatalá, my father, has given permission for rum to be drunk in honor of Shangó today."

"That's sure to make a lot of people happy," replied Andres impishly.

The dish of the night was rooster in wine sauce. Earlier, santeros had offered the blood of dozens of roosters in sacrifice to Shangó. Many implements that needed to "eat," or be infused with ashé through sacrifice, were "fed" the blood of the roosters. Now it was time to consume the flesh of the sacrificed animals. After everyone had eaten, the three batá drummers began to play as a specially trained singer praised the orishas. The long tables where everyone had feasted were removed, and the whole backyard became a temple where everyone danced for the orishas. When the singer intoned one of the ancient Lucumí chants in praise of Shangó, the whole crowd joined in the chorus:

Caboé, Caboé
Caboé, Cabiosile o

Be welcome, be welcome
Be welcome, my lord.

A young girl of about fifteen, Andres' niece, began to tremble violently. Someone made a motion to assist her, but Zena shouted, "Don't touch her!" Barbarita, as the girl was called, jumped up and fell hard on the ground; she then sprang up with eyes bulging, her face transformed. Her dancing was now brusque, manly. She swung an invisible sword or axe. The crowd became ecstatic. Shouts of welcome to the orisha resonated throughout the ilé. "Shangó 'ta 'qui!" "Cabiosile, Baba-mí!" (Shangó is here! Welcome, my lord and father!) The song to Obatalá also had satisfactory results; the greatest of all orishas descended from heaven to commune with mortals. Amanda became rigid; then a steady trembling like the passage of a strong electrical current began to come over her. Fully possessed by the divine Obatalá, Amanda danced a slow, stately dance that transfixed those present. "Obatalá 'ta 'qui!" (Obatalá is here!) A great circle formed around Amanda/Obatalá. The orisha began to single out certain individuals for counseling. "You must watch your husband, he is seeing another woman," Obatalá told a startled young woman. "Ask my *caballo* [Amanda] later what to do to keep him from leaving you." Pointing to another woman's stomach, Obatalá said, "You have a tumor right there. Tell my *caballo* to give you some omiero to drink and then go to the white man's doctor to get an operation. Don't worry, you'll be fine afterward."

As I watched, fascinated, Obatalá turned to where my mother stood and asked her, "Daughter of Shangó, why haven't you given me the boy yet? He must be *asentado* [fully initiated] before the year is out." Looking down at me, Obatalá smiled and picked me up; with his face right in front of mine, he said, "You are my son, my true son. I brought you to this world and I'll never leave you." Obatalá then hugged me, inundating me with such a feeling of well-being that I could not contain my tears of happiness. How fortunate are the santeros! While others pray to an invisible god hoping someday to see him, the Divine is manifested in Santeria as living, breathing beings one can touch, kiss, love.

Amanda's bembé to Shangó was a total success. Eight or nine orishas descended from heaven to counsel those present. Mother and I stayed over as Zena's houseguests, sleeping on straw mats.

As the night passed the bullfrogs became silent and were replaced by an orchestra of crickets. The cool breeze of the wee hours brought in the mellifluous aroma of a nearby orange grove. Through the square opening that served as a window, the little boy that I was could see stars as huge as those in the Van Gogh print hanging in my father's office. The sky had turned a deep, dark blue; Shangó must have ceded it to Yemayá, the great mother goddess of Santeria, whose emblematic color is as blue as the seven seas she rules. When sleep finally defeated my childish excitement, I dreamt of a place far away where the god-king Shangó ruled and where men and spirits comingled, a place far removed from El Vedado.

--- NOTES ---

1. Cuban society is basically triracial; light-skinned blacks (mulattos) often consider themselves a separate group from the whites and the blacks. See Carlos Moore's "Congo or Carabali? Race Relations in Socialist Cuba," *Caribbean Review* XV, no. 2 (Spring 1986) 12–16.

2. Cuban santeros celebrate the feast of Obatalá on September 24. This is the same day as the Catholic feast of Our Lady of Mercy, which provides the public "face" of Obatalá. In Santeria, children born with the caul are said to belong to Obatalá.

CHAPTER 2

LEGACY

My father's European forebears have been carefully researched by my uncle, the genealogist Jorge Canizares; they include a number of aristocratic personages. I find, however, that my mother's side of the family, though not nearly as "distinguished," is infinitely more colorful. Coming as they do from such divergent backgrounds, it is surprising that my mother and father may have an ancestor in common; my father's legitimate grandfather, the Count Brunet, may be my mother's illegitimate great-grandfather.

Around 1870, fifteen-year-old Maria was a house slave in the service of the Count Brunet, the principal landowner in the Cuban city of Trinidad. Maria's mother, Francisca, was a Lucumí (Yoruba) born in the African city-state of Oyo. Francisca had been with the count's family for many years. The count had given Maria to his elderly driver, José Pérez, as a wife. José was a freedman fiercely loyal to the count. He was born in Arará (probably modern Benin). In 1870 Maria gave birth to a boy on December 4, a day associated in Cuban Santeria with the thunder god Shangó. The baby bore a purple birthmark on his tongue in the shape of a double-edged axe, a sure sign of the true sons of Shangó—in fact, some santeros contend that such children are actually incarnations of the orisha. Some of the old blacks in the count's household saw in the baby's red hair another sign of Shangó's predilection for the child, red being Shangó's emblematic color. Less pious observers remembered that the count's gray hair had been red in his youth.

The boy was christened José but was called Bangoché, a name traditionally given to Shangó's chosen sons. Bangocheíto—diminutive of Bangoché—received an elementary education because he was allowed to attend classes with the white children of the count's household. Bangocheíto received training as a tailor, but soon his natural gift for fortune-telling and healing made him a relatively prosperous *curandero*, or healer. In the summer of 1890, the count gave Bangocheíto a small property just outside Trinidad, where he set up his practice as a *curandero*. The attractive young man soon began to negatively affect the business of Andrea Ortiz, Trinidad's most famous *bruja* (witch).

Andrea Ortiz was a peculiar woman. A native of the Canary Islands, she had come to Cuba under mysterious circumstances— her grandson, German Pérez, now in his eighties and living in New York, tells me in all seriousness that Andrea flew to the New World on a broomstick. "I saw her flying around her hut when I was a kid," German told me as he crossed himself, his eyes still reflecting a terror experienced three quarters of a century before. My own grandmother, Andrea Isabel, who was named for her grandmother Andrea Ortiz, was so afraid of the witch that for her entire life she refused to utter her own name, calling herself Ophelia instead. My grandmother also claimed that she had witnessed Andrea's peculiar air show as a child.

Very tall, big boned, and thin, with an ashen complexion, hypnotic pale gray eyes, and graying yellow hair tightly pulled back in a bun, Andrea Ortiz was striking, though not really attractive. Her long, straight nose and thin, tightly pressed lips gave her a stern, angry look. Then in her forties, she lived alone with her four children, two boys and two girls, in a hut at the end of a long, winding cobblestone road. Down the hill, at the beginning of that same road, was Bangocheíto's shop. Soon the town was ablaze with rumors of the impending showdown between the Canary Islands witch and the young Lucumí upstart. One day, Bangocheíto received the message he had been expecting: "Andrea challenges you to go to her place if you dare, but she warns that you will never come out." Bangocheíto's followers begged him not to go meet the *bruja,* but he laughed their fears off, saying, "I'll show that old woman a thing or two! She'll have to take her broom and fly the hell out of Trinidad—this town is mine!"

Bangocheíto took up the challenge and climbed the hill to the *bruja*'s hut. The totally unexpected outcome of the dreaded meeting still brings a wry smile to German Pérez's face: "In a way my grandmother was right, for Bangocheíto never left her house. They became lovers and remained so till the day he died thirty years later." "Theirs was a classic love story," continues German. "They overcame their differences in backgrounds, in ages, and most important, in races. In those days race relations in Cuba were less than cordial, especially in the city of Trinidad [see Appendix]. It was very rare for a white woman to live with a colored man, but Andrea was some woman! They never experienced prejudism [*sic*]."

Even though Andrea was too old to bear children according to nineteenth-century standards, she and Bangocheíto had four—three girls and a boy. One of the girls, Juana (my great-grandmother), was a priestess of Shangó like her father. Although hereditary priesthoods to particular orishas is a feature of Yoruba religion that did not survive in Cuba, the custom was kept alive in Bangocheíto's family for many years; it is said that all of Bangocheíto's ancestors in Oyo had been priests and priestesses of Shangó. The tradition was broken when Obatalá wrestled my head away from Shangó, and I became the first in the line not to be a priest of the thunder god.

At his death, Bangocheíto bequeathed his *libreta* (notebook or diary) to his daughter Juana, who left it to her eldest daughter, Andrea Isabel. Today, that beautifully written treasure of information is in the possession of my aunt Haydée in Havana.

In 1905 Juana, eldest of Bangocheíto's daughters, became the common-law wife of a small landowner of Spanish and Amerindian ancestry named Feliciáno Zayas Tardio. He was a good, respectable man who had wanted to divorce his first wife, an impossibility at that time. The thirty-year-old man and his fifteen-year-old common-law wife lived as a married couple and were accepted as such. Three girls were born of that happy union, which ended tragically after fifteen years when, following a boundary dispute, Feliciáno accepted a poisoned drink from a feuding neighbor who pretended to want peace. Feliciáno's legal wife, whom nobody had heard from in fifteen years, showed up at the funeral, laying claim to Feliciáno's substantial estate. Juana and her three daughters found themselves literally out on the street. Juana moved to Havana, where she eked out an existence as a washerwoman. Juana's eldest daughter, Andrea Isabel (called Ophelia), eloped at the age of eleven with a destitute son of Spaniards named Valentin Gonzalez y Gonzalez; they had two children, my mother, Ana Rosa (who later took the stage name Roxana), and my aunt Haydée. Like her mother, Ophelia's itá (set of rules, taboos, and predictions established at the time of a person's initiation) had forbidden her from profiting from the practice of Santeria, so her priesthood remained a private affair.

My grandmother had begun to experience doubts about initiating her two daughters into Santeria, for she was leery of how some santeros less talented than herself were becoming wealthy in Havana while her own santos kept her in extreme poverty. She had also begun to dream of a better life for her white-looking daughters, and the fact that Santeria was viewed as a social hindrance by the wealthy people whose clothes she washed did not escape her. When my mother was three years old, however, she heard the drumming of a Santeria feast in a nearby house and, running away from her mother, entered the bembé, where Shangó possessed her little body and did not leave it until certain preliminary initiatory rites were performed.

At the age of ten my mother won a national radio talent show, launching a career in entertainment—radio, nightclubs, movies, and television—that was to last forty years. Her success, which she attributed to her santos, gave her access to a social class she could not have entered otherwise. Once, when her career was beginning to take off, my mother was offered a lucrative contract to tour South and Central America with a troupe that included a singing and dancing group known as Las Platinadas de Oscar Moreno. This first trip out of Cuba would supposedly internationalize my mother's fame, and her agent was adamant that she should accept it. But when she was about to board the plane, a serious-looking black youth of about twelve, neatly dressed in black slacks and a red shirt, approached her and told her, "Señora, don't go." My mother refused to board the plane, even though her luggage was already on board. The impressario tried to coax my mother onto the plane; he became very annoyed when she refused and finally fired her. The next day, the entire country was shocked to hear the news of a plane crash that had ended the lives of many bright, talented people. To this day my mother believes Eleggua materialized and saved her life, for in one of his manifestations he is said to be an eternal child and his emblematic colors are red and black.

As my mother ascended the ladder of social and artistic success, she hid her adherence to Santeria from most of her new friends. In private, she continued to perform Santeria rituals and believed her santos were responsible for her fame and fortune. My mother's three successive marriages to prominent men—Jewish-Canadian millionaire Benny Hammer, Mexican entertainer Guillermo Chazaro (son of Mexico's best-loved singer, Toña la Negra), and wealthy physician Raul Canizares-Verson, Count Brunet—cemented her position in Havana's upper class. But she hid even from her husbands the fact that she was a priestess of Shangó. After separating from my father when I was seven (they would remarry twenty years later) my mother felt free to more openly practice Santeria, allowing the elder santeros who had guided her spiritual life to initiate me into the mysteries of santo. It was in their ilés that I learned the magical, centuries-old stories of the orishas and became an integral part of their world.

My family's history shows the complex, sometimes contradictory attitudes of Cubans toward Santeria. The next chapter explores the customs and institutions that shaped Santeria's evolution in Cuban society.

CHAPTER 3

EVOLUTION AND SURVIVAL OF SANTERIA

Yoruba soy, lloro en yoruba,
lucumí.
Como soy un yoruba de Cuba,
quiero que hasta Cuba suba mi llanto yoruba;
que suba el alegre llanto yoruba
que sale de mi.

I am a Yoruba, in Yoruba I weep,
in Lucumí.
A Yoruba from Cuba,

I send to Cuba my Yoruba cry,
the joyous Yoruba weeping
which springs forth from me.

"Son no. 6" by Nicolas Guillen,
Cuba's national poet

More than any other African group in Cuba, the descendants of the
Yoruba have been particularly successful in retaining impressive
amounts of their culture, influencing the character of Cuba itself
in what the great Cuban anthropologist Fernando Ortiz called a
transculturation process. In his book *Cuban Counterpoint,* Ortiz
describes a Cuba whose history is shaped by its two most important
exports: sugar and tobacco.[1] Each of these products, according to
Ortiz, plays a sometimes dissonant, sometimes harmonious counterpoint on the musical instrument that is Cuba. White sugar and brown
tobacco serve as excellent metaphors for the two principal racial
components of the island, the European (Spanish) and the African
(Lucumí, Congo, Carabali). These two races blend in curious, surprising ways, painting the Cuban landscape in subtle, sometimes
beautiful, sometimes violent polychromatic hues. The result is a
Cuba at times dissonant, at times harmonious, full of contradictions,
yet remarkably cohesive.

As Fidel Castro once noted, Cuba is an Afro-Hispanic rather than
a Latin American country. Although race relations between blacks,
whites, and mulattos have been tumultuous (see Appendix), there
is no denying the pervasive influence African culture in general—
and Yoruba culture in particular—has had on such areas of Cuban
society as language, music, and religion. For example, Cubans call
twins *jimaquas,* while most other Spanish-speaking countries use
the words *gemelos* or *mellizos.* Recently a Cuban-born professor
of Spanish argued with me that *jimaquas* was a good Spanish word;
only after a futile search in her huge Spanish dictionary did she
admit that she had no idea where the word comes from. As Lydia
Cabrera has noted, when aristocratic white families in Cuba announced the birth of their *jimaquas,* they did not realize they were
using a word of Yoruba origin.

Ernesto Lecuona, Cuba's greatest musical composer, created lyric Spanish pieces such as "Malagueña." He was also, however, a master of Cuban rhythms. His cousin Margarita Lecuona, a renowned composer in her own right, created what may be Cuba's most famous Afro song, "Babalú," popularized in the United States by Dési Arnaz. African influences, then, while rarely acknowledged, define the Cuban ethos.

Even Cuban Catholic piety has been influenced by Africa. Our Lady of Charity, designated guardian of Cuba by Pius XII, is often pictured as a beautiful *mulata*. Many of the old ladies of "pure" Spanish blood who vigorously shake yellow handkerchiefs above their heads as a salute to the Virgin do not realize they are engaging in an ancient Lucumí salute to Oshún, whose emblematic color is yellow and who has been identified in Cuba with Our Lady of Charity. Santeria, then, just like African culture in general, has remained underground, but its contributions to the Cuban ethos in music, language, and folklore are immeasurable.

THE CABILDOS

In Cuba, as in Brazil, the Yoruba found a fortunate confluence of factors that allowed them to retain much of their culture. Two institutions in Cuba unwittingly converged to make this possible: Spanish ethnic clubs and the Roman Catholic Church. Spanish colonialists in Cuba were not a homogeneous group; they came from Galicia, Vizcaya, Asturias, Andalusia, and the Canary Islands. They spoke Gallego, Catalan, and Basque, as well as the official Castillian Spanish. Each one of these groups formed its own social clubs and mutual aid societies along ethnic, regional, and linguistic lines. Unlike their English-speaking counterparts, Spanish and Portuguese slaveowners encouraged the development of ethnic factions among their slaves, thinking that in this manner they would remain divided and not unite against them. Under the auspices of the Church, ostensibly to Christianize the Africans, slaves and free blacks were allowed to organize their own social clubs and mutual aid societies; these societies, called *cabildos*, were mirror images of the Spanish clubs and were also organized along ethnic, regional, and linguistic lines. There is documentary evidence that by 1568 there were already African clubs called cabildos in Havana—some still said to be in operation in revolutionary Cuba. Soon the cabildos developed a unique function as a place where the "old traditions" of Africa could be preserved.[2]

The religious function of the cabildos as repositories of African religious beliefs eventually became the dominant characteristic of these clubs. Although many distinct African traditions were preserved in the cabildos, the Yoruba/Lucumí religion probably benefited the most from them. Three great traditions, each attached to particular linguistic groups, have survived to this day among Afro-Cubans: the Palo Monte and Palo Mayombe traditions of the Bantu-speaking so-called Congo people; the Abakuá/Ñáñigo societies of the Efik-speaking Carabalí; and the Lucumí or Santería religion of the Yoruba-speaking Lucumí. Other smaller groups, such as the Fon (called Arará in Cuba), were also able to retain their customs. Arguably the Lucumí best adapted their way of life to the Cuban environment. The reason for the success of Santeria may in fact lie in its intrinsic similarity to popular forms of Catholicism, especially the worship of the saints.

European Catholicism never eradicated its "pagan" precursors. Even as orthodox a Catholic country as Ireland still shows vestiges of pre-Christian religion in its forms of worship; for example, it is widely believed that Saint Bridget is a Christianized celtic goddess.[3] In popular Catholicism, the fine line between the worship due only to God and the veneration accorded his saints has often been blurry. Slaves watched as their white masters prostrated themselves in front of images of saints, offering them flowers and lighting candles in front of them as a way of thanking the images for petitions granted. Saint Barbara, for example, the patron saint of soldiers, was thought to have the power to send down lightning from heaven. The astute Africans seized the opportunity to keep alive their ancient deities, the orishas, by deliberately disguising them as Catholic saints; Shangó, the orisha of lightning, was linked with Saint Barbara.

SECRECY AND SURVIVAL

Despite Santeria's integration into Cuban society, the majority of Cuban santeros still adhere to the long-standing customs of not talking candidly to outsiders, of cloaking their faith with Catholic trappings. Traditionally, even family members did not know that their own relatives were active in Santeria. In my own family my father, of an upper-class white background, thought of Santeria as the backward religion of an uncivilized people. He did not realize that one of his sisters, his wife, and his only son were initiated in the religion. This attitude of secrecy is changing, especially in multiethnic ilés. The non-Cuban santeros are increasingly questioning the dissimulation component of Santeria.

The reluctance of many Cubans to publicly acknowledge allegiance to Santeria has a complicated, convoluted history. At the heart of the matter is the fact that Santeria, along with other African-based religions, is associated with a group once thought to be subhuman by the dominant, white, Catholic Cuban society—African slaves. This, however, cannot account for the continuing reluctance of many Santeria participants to publicly proclaim their faith, even in a country like the United States where religious freedom is guaranteed. Santeria's reliance on animal sacrifices, deemed a barbaric practice by many Americans—even those who eat meat—is another reason why some santeros are reluctant to discuss their faith with outsiders. A much more intriguing reason I have heard given for not wishing to be publicly identified as a practitioner has to do with the values, or rather the lack of values, some people (including some santeros) feel exists in Santeria.

The theme of the "closet" practitioner of African-based religions is a recurring one in Cuban society. Famed Cuban entertainer Beny More is a case in point. Universally acclaimed as Cuba's best popular singer, he would be called a superstar in today's parlance. Beny's close friends often tried to find out if he belonged to any of the Afro-Cuban religions. Beny usually denied having ties to the Afro-Cuban religious world, although his mother was pure Lucumí. After Beny's death, many people were shocked to find out he had been a leader of the dreaded Abakuá society, the Náñigos who Cuban children are taught to fear much as American children fear the boogeyman.

————————————— NOTES —————————————

1. Fernando Ortiz, *Cuban Counterpoint* (New York: Alfred A. Knopf, 1947).

2. For a thorough study of the Cuban cabildos of the nineteenth century, see Philip Anthony Howard, *Culture, Nationalism, and Liberation: The Afro-Cuban Mutual Aid Societies in the Nineteenth Century* (Ph.D. diss., Indiana University, 1986).

3. For more on the relationship between St. Bridget and goddess worship, see Mary Condren, *The Serpent and the Goddess: Women, Religion and Power in Celtic Ireland* (San Francisco: Harper & Row, 1989.

CHAPTER 4

HIERARCHY

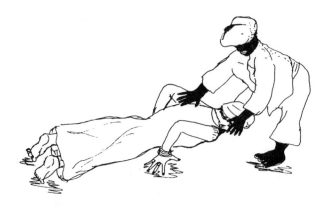

The initiatic life is like a rainbow: each color or phase change releases a distinctly new quality from the continuum of being. Further initiations continue to break the bounds of fear and limitation, opening the door to the spiritual and metaphysical levels of existence.[1]

Involvement in Santeria follows a carefully developed hierarchical structure, which must be understood to discuss the religion in any depth. This hierarchical model is based on the amount of involvement and type of initiation a participant has undergone. I contend that, as a person ascends the Santeria hierarchy, he or she begins to understand the religion in a different manner. A shift in perspective occurs, moving from a Eurocentric to an African worldview and understanding. This shift is closely linked to the use of dissimulation in representing Santeria.

Very broadly—and somewhat arbitrarily—participation in Santeria can be broken down into the following groupings, in ascending order of importance: interested observers; occasional clients; habitual clients; amulet recipients; Eleggua initiates; guerreros initiates; collares initiates; and the two types I refer to as "high-level" initiates, santeros and babalaos. This is admittedly a simplified schema, for there also are numerous subdivisions, such as oriaté and italero. For clarity's sake, however, I will concentrate on the major divisions I have listed.

Interested Observers   These range from the curious who like to read about Santeria to the more serious investigators, like scholars, who nevertheless remain outside the tradition.

Occasional Clients   These people seek out the Santeria practitioner for professional reasons just as they would use the services of a psychologist or a physician; they patronize the santero or santera in order to obtain a desired result. The services provided might be curing a health problem, giving advice in important decisions, or seeing into the future. Occasional clients do not need to have an interest in Santeria as a religion, just as they may use the services of a physician without being interested in medicine. Most occasional clients are unaware of Santeria's distinctiveness vis-à-vis Catholicism, believing that the santero or santera is Catholic. This is reinforced by the santero's use of Catholic images and by the language, common to popular Catholicism, employed by the practitioner: "We'll light a candle to Saint Barbara" or "Saint Francis will help us."

Habitual Clients   Habitual clients are usually aware of Santeria's distinctive character but do not consider themselves to be part of Santeria. However, they do make use of a Santeria practitioner's services regularly. In Cuban society, many prominent people would not make a move without first consulting with their santero.

Amulet Recipients   Some physical objects, sometimes termed fetishes, can be conferred on nonsanteros. Called by various names—resguardos, guardieros, amuletos—these demand a certain commitment to Santeria, since they require ritualistic treatment periodically in order to remain efficacious. People who accept these amulets do so in order to gain some reward, such as improved luck, protection from evil spirits, or sexual attractiveness. Because these amulets require priestly ministering from time to time, the people who have them sometimes begin to think of themselves as belonging to the ilé (house or spiritual community) of the Santeria priest or priestess who gave—or more usually sold—them an amulet.

Eleggua Initiates Generally a figure of Eleggua—not to be confused with "making Eleggua," discussed below—is given at the same time the guerreros initiation is performed. Often, however, this protective orisha is conferred alone. Eleggua is a mischievous, childlike, theriomorphic figure in the Yoruba/Santeria pantheon. Both loved and feared, he is an orisha of vast importance. He has many manifestations, more than any other orisha. Eleggua is the Lord of the Crossroads, a title that alludes to the orisha's control over people's destinies. As Guardian of the Gates, Eleggua protects homes and opens the gates of opportunity for those he favors. Eleggua is also God's messenger and as such is the only orisha other than the great Obatalá to know the secret place where God Almighty, Olodumare, resides. Because of all his attributes, wherever the orisha are revered, Eleggua is the first orisha to be propitiated. Keeping Eleggua happy is a major concern of all santeros.

Both santeros and babalaos can confer Eleggua, though purists insist those given by babalaos are stronger. The usual Eleggua figure is a stone or cement "head" about six inches high with eyes, nose, mouth, and ears fashioned out of cowrie shells. Other Eleggua figures are made out of large seashells and coconuts (coconut Elegguas are often temporary). The Eleggua figures are "stuffed" with secret ingredients thought to give them life and are also periodically sprinkled with sacrificial blood to strengthen their power. A person who has an Eleggua cannot consider him- or herself a casual participant in Santeria. Eleggua needs to be propitiated each Monday morning in a ritualistic fashion, including the recitation of prayers in Lucumí. Offerings such as smoked *jutía* (a possumlike rodent), candy, toasted corn, toys, and cigar smoke, as well as rum sprayed from the believer's mouth directly on the figure, are to be given to Eleggua without fail, for the orisha is quick to close the doors on those who do not propitiate him in a responsible manner. The Eleggua figure is usually kept inside a small cabinet behind the home's main doorway. (Once an Anglo friend asked me why we Cubans keep our night tables behind our doors instead of by our beds!) Having an Eleggua is a responsibility. Propitiate him and he will open your doorways; neglect him and you will suffer.

Guerreros Initiates Aside from Eleggua, the orishas known as warriors are Ogún, ruler of iron and of hard labor; Ochosi, lord of the hunt; and Ósun, an ambiguous figure sometimes considered a minor orisha or a nature spirit. There is disagreement over whether the guerreros or the collares initiation is more important, but short of becoming fully initiated as a santero or santera, these two initiations are the most important and involved. A person acquires guerreros to defend him- or herself from material as well as spiritual enemies, but the guerreros is usually seen as an initial initiation for people on the way to becoming fully initiated as santeras or santeros. Traditionally only babalaos can confer this initiation, although lately a "babalao-free" Santeria seems to be emerging in many parts of the United States, one where the santeros do much of their work without needing a babalao. The guerreros receives objects representing the orishas associated with the new rank: Ogún is a small cauldron filled with iron tools, Ochosi is an iron bow and arrow, and Ósun is a little rooster on top of what looks like a stylized iron chalice but may in fact be an adaptation of a staff used by Yoruba magicians in Africa. These warriors—along with Eleggua—are usually propitiated on Mondays.

Collares Initiates   This is a very important initiation in Santeria for several reasons, one of which is that wearing of the multicolored beaded necklaces—collares—of the orishas publicly identifies the wearer as a believer in Santeria. In some ilés, people who have been initiated as both guerreros and collares are considered to be "half-seated" santeros, implying that half of the requirements for full initiation have been fulfilled. The necklaces are usually—but not always—given by women. To prepare the necklaces, complex ceremonies involving several priests or priestesses are required. The actual ceremony in which a person receives the collares—called *elekes* in Lucumí—is very involved; the collares recipient is ritually bathed and must shed his or her old clothes for new white ones. The lengthy prayers and incantations of the "putting on the necklaces" ceremony are unmistakably African.

To prepare the collares, each necklace is ritually washed in an herbal infusion consisting of water and the sacred herbs of each of the orishas represented. The string used in the collares must be cotton or some other absorbent material (never nylon), for sacrificial blood must be absorbed through the thread, to charge the necklace with ashé. The color patterns of each necklace indicate which orisha is being represented. The first necklace to be conferred is usually, but not always, that of Eleggua, who as the Lord of the Gate opens each Santeria ceremony; Eleggua's necklace is made of alternating black and red beads. A few ilés give Obatalá's all-white necklace first, since Obatalá is the greatest of all orishas. The number of collares given at the ceremony varies slightly, and santeros may keep on adding necklaces as needed. Most of the time, however, the first five necklaces conferred are Eleggua, Obatalá, Yemayá, Shangó, and Oshún. Other orishas commonly represented are Ogún and Babalú Ayé.

Technically speaking, collares initiates are not santeros (priests), yet at this stage many people consider their religion to be Santeria. A person with the rank of collares initiate has the orishas' constant protection. Collares are often given to people destined to become santeros who do not yet have the financial means to undergo the costly kariocha, or full initiation ceremony, which in the United States can cost from $5,000 to $50,000 or more, depending on which orisha is to be "made."

Santeros   Although believers in Santeria are often referred to as santeros, this is a technical term meaning "priests." In the emerging "new Santeria" of the United States all comers are encouraged to undergo full initiation, but in traditional Cuban Santeria only those few whose heads have been claimed by an orisha should undergo the kariocha (Lucumí for "to seat on the head") initiation.

After a lengthy period of preparation, traditionally three years more or less—in the United States, because of the faster pace of U.S. society, it can be as short as three months—those called to be santeros undergo an extremely complex initiation involving several highly trained practitioners. The culmination of the ceremony, which is also called *asiento* or *hacer santo* ("making saint"), is a three-day feast during which the neophyte is presented to the community as a new brother or sister. In Cuba, it was usually at this time that the orisha that had been "seated" first possessed the neophyte. Actual orisha possession, obligatory in Cuban Santeria, is becoming rarer in America, possibly because consecrated batá drums, which have to be played for the orishas to possess the neophyte, are also very rare.

After initiation, both males and females are known by the feminine name *iyabó* (in Yoruba, *iyawó*), which literally means "bride" but is understood in Santeria to mean "novice." During the one-year novitiate that follows, iyabós must wear white and observe numerous taboos, some of which they must continue to respect for the rest of their lives. These taboos, as well as the course the neophyte must take in his or her new life as a santero or santera, is contained in the itá, an important divination, made by a specially trained senior santero known as an italero, which basically tells the novice what his or her future is going to be like. Some people who may anticipate setting up a lucrative practice as a Santeria practitioner after initiation may be told during the itá that they cannot profit from the practice of Santeria.

During their year as iyabós santeros also learn the technical and practical aspects of their new status as fully initiated priests or priestesses. These include learning to make magic potions, learning to cast cowrie shells for divination, and learning Lucumí (at least enough for ritual purposes)—as well as learning to look at the world in a different manner, often involving a shift in perspective from European to traditional African. At this time, many santeros also shift their values from those of the Catholic Church to those of Yoruba traditions. I still recall my amazement when, during my novitiate, my old padrino, my godfather in Santeria, told me that Our Lady of Mercy, whom I had been taught to venerate as Obatalá, was not really Obatalá. Many marginal participants in Santeria, as well as some mid-level initiates, hold the belief that African orishas and Catholic saints are the same entities with different names. When scholars, such as Melville Herskovits, investigate the religion, this is often the point of view they are exposed to, one that leads to the conclusion that Santeria is syncretistic.

When I was seven, during my novitiate, I was praying in front of an image of Our Lady of Mercy when Padrino approached me and asked me what I was doing. "Praying to Obatalá," I said. The old man slowly lifted his eyes to the statue and then lowered them to meet mine, saying softly, "No, my son, that is not Obatalá." Taking me back to the room where he kept the soup tureens used in Santeria to hide the fundamental stones of the orishas, Padrino lifted the lid of the white soup tureen that held Obatalá's sacred stones. He said, in a voice filled with emotion, "This is Obatalá!" Watching my puzzled expression, Padrino added, smiling, "Obatalá can only be in the *otán* [stones] and in here," gently tapping my head with his finger. This was the first inkling I had that Santeria is deliberately syncretic, as opposed to unconsciously so.

Babalaos In Santeria, babalaos (from the Yoruba *babalawo,* Father of the Mystery) are considered the high priests of the religion. In Cuba, babalaos always undergo initiation as santeros before becoming priests of the powerful orisha Ifá; this road is only open to men after the call to become babalaos appears in their itá. Only men of good character can become babalaos. This is rather unusual, since Santeria tends not to be judgmental in a traditional Western sense. Homosexuals, women, and spirit mediums are barred from becoming babalaos.

Babalaos are essential to many Santeria rituals. They are usually the ones who are trained to kill four-footed animals. (One stereotype of Santeria that is true is that chickens are the most common sacrificial victims. Rarely, and only when specialists do it, are four-footed animals sacrificed.) The ceremony through which a man becomes a babalao is called "making ifá." In Cuba Ifá, a name of the orisha Orula in Africa, is usually applied to the ceremony, not the orisha.

Making ifá is the most secretive initiation ceremony in Santeria; anyone who undergoes the initiation must promise never to reveal the particulars of what he experiences. The process was a total mystery to all but babalaos until a former babalao-turned-Communist, Gabriel Pasos, exposed the details of his own initiation in an attempt to ingratiate himself with the Communist party in Cuba. He told his story to a sociologist Party member, Lourdes Lopez, who published it in 1975 as a book, *Estudio de un babalao.*[2] My own sources confirm the accuracy of Pasos' account, and I rely heavily on it here.

The initiation process fills a week, during which the initiate has no contact with the outside world. He spends this time in the company of the babalaos from the surrounding area who have come together to initiate and welcome a new member to their fraternity. These babalaos lead the initiate through ritual cleansings, force him to endure specific punishments, and teach him secrets of divination, including the *oddus* of the Book of Ifá. The emphasis of the week's activities is on the initiate renouncing his former self, accepting the responsibility of his new position, and taking his place with his fellow babalaos.

More than any other Santeria initiation, making ifá is steeped in the spirit of its African roots. Communication is almost exclusively in Lucumí—and partially in a veiled Lucumí that eavesdropping outsiders cannot understand. For example, early during the initiation the aspirant is asked to declare his intentions and sincerity about becoming a babalao. While he stands outside the Oddua room, the inner sanctum where the sacred Olofi artifact is kept, a senior babalao calls to him:

> *Erin kakole keke*
> *agno orun agno opon*
> *kilebache Olofin tiuyo timi*
> *erin kakole keke.*

According to babalao Paco Cuevas, this means:

> *May the four winds take you away*
> *if your oaths to God and the holy table of Ifá*
> *and your oaths to Almighty God*
> *you are not able to keep.*
> *May the four winds take you away.*

The kneeling aspirant must reply:

> *Erin kakole leile*
> *kinche Olofi nilu anmego.*
>
> *The four winds are my banners,*
> *for I, one of God's people, will follow*
> *the counsel of my elders.*

Some of the individual rites emphasize the babalaos' identification with the legendary first sixteen kings of Yoruba. One of these is the "receiving of Orula," probably the most important part of the seven-day ceremony, which takes place on the first day. The initiate has been shaved, painted, and crowned with a headdress of coconut shell, beads, and red parrot feathers. One of the senior babalaos, often his padrino, paints the names or symbols of the sixteen kings on a long block of cedar that is laid before the initiate, and the five senior babalaos then paint their symbols on the block to show that they witnessed the event. After this, twenty-one palm nuts, or *ikines*, are taken from a gourd filled with river water or rainwater and placed on each of the twenty-one symbols; they are then coated with the feathers and blood of two black hens that are sacrificed. The padrino then dresses each *ikin* with a mixture of honey, cocoa butter, palm oil, and small pieces of coconut pulp. He says, "This is the great truth of our faith: behold Orula, make him part of your soul." The initiate, with his hands behind his back, must use his mouth to take up each *ikin*, clean it by swallowing the stuff that covers it, and spit the *ikin* back into the water filled gourd. By doing this he has taken Orula's ashé into his soul and is now considered a neophyte babalao. This ceremony is followed by the "pact with Death" in which, accompanied by ritual dances and songs, the babalao makes a deal with Death that he will not touch his head without permission from Orula himself.

As a Santeria believer becomes more involved in the religion, the initiaic process brings new spiritual awareness and sense of connection to Africa. Imbued with the powerful spirit of African ancestors and the vital force of the orishas, Santeria initiates bring to their modern, urban environments the magic and balance of African wisdom. Many santeros feel that in the competitive world of the West this ancient wisdom brings them peace and balance, which give them an edge in not only surviving but thriving under pressure.

NOTES

1. Robert Lawlor, *Voices of the First Day* (Rochester, Vermont: Inner Traditions International, 1991), 194.

2. Lourdes Lopez, *Estudio de un* babalao (Havana: Universidad de la Havana, 1975).

CHAPTER 5

SYNCRETISM OR DISSIMULATION?

Cuban Santeria is one of the Afro-American (South, Central, and North American) religious expressions often termed *syncretic.* Other examples are Haitian Vodun and Brazilian Candonblé. In this context syncretism generally means the unconscious, uncritical adoption of the dominant culture's religious beliefs. I believe that the process of aligning Santeria beliefs was less a case of syncretism than of dissimulation—the conscious, deliberate use of elements of Catholicism to allow people to practice their beliefs undisturbed. Building on those findings of other scholars that my training as a santero validates as correct, I have devised a model that demonstrates how the dissimulation/deception component functions within the framework of Santeria.

Although syncretism is a fluid term with several meanings, I am applying it here according to Melville Herskovits' specific definition: "The acculturative process . . . [by which] a synthesis between aboriginal African patterns and the European traditions to which [the negroes] have been exposed [is achieved]."[1]

Herskovits popularized the term *syncretism,* referring to Afro-American cultures, in his pioneering 1937 article "African Gods and Catholic Saints in New World Negro Belief."[2] He used the word *syncretism* interchangeably with *synthesis.* According to Herskovits, such syncretism can be seen in Santeria's African orisha/Catholic saint correspondences.[3] Herskovits saw evidence of this rather simple synthesis in the fact that, according to him, Africans in Cuba, Haiti, and Brazil thought of themselves as Catholic while at the same time they belonged to "fetish cults."[4] However, Herskovits' description of Santeria as a synthesis of African and Catholic elements "misses the creative and self-conscious decisions that underlie Santeria syncretism," as Joseph Murphy has noted.[5]

Herskovits' perspective is still shared by a significant number of modern scholars. Following Herskovits' model, Juan J. Sosa defines Santeria as "the worship of African gods as Catholic saints, a result of the transculturation process of the Cuban people and the religious syncretism [resulting from] such a process. . . ."[6]

Another modern writer on Santeria who, as Isidoro Andres Pérez y Mena correctly points out, has a "Herskovits-oriented interpretation of syncretism"[7] is Migene González-Wippler, who has written copiously—but with varying degrees of success—on Santeria. The noted French anthropologist Roger Bastide understood the Catholic saint/African orisha identifications differently from Herskovits. For Bastide, the Catholic masks served to identify certain aspects of the protean orishas with Catholic equivalents.[8] As Murphy has noted in his remarkable book on Santeria, Bastide's ideas of "mosaic syncretism" and "symbiosis" are more specific than "mere mixture" and more complex than a simple fusion of religious traditions.[9]

The way in which Bastide summarizes how devotees view the

relationship between Catholic and African elements in their lives
comes closer to my own perspective than Herskovits' model does:

> In essence . . . there is only one universal . . . God and
> creator. However, this God is too remote from mankind
> for the latter to enter into direct contact with Him:
> therefore "intermediaries" are necessary—Catholic saints
> or angels of the Old Testament for Europeans, orisha or
> vodun for the Negroes . . . such variations are not fun-
> damental. In any case, one can always "translate" one
> . . . into another.[10]

What I would add to Bastide is that the "translation," as it is
occurring, may be more for the benefit of the outsider. In other
words, a santero's statement that "orishas are the same as saints"
may be understood as attempts by the devotee to make his or her
world understandable and concrete to the outsider through the use
of analogous imagery.

Coming back to Herskovits, whose contributions to this question
are invaluable, I propose that his model must be reinterpreted and
reevaluated, particularly as it pertains to Santeria. Herskovits'
description of Santeria as a synthesis of African traditions and
popular Catholicism fails to take into account the deliberate disguising of Lucumí orishas as Catholic saints—an act I propose was
fully intentional—with the goal of using Catholic saints as masks in
order to preserve the African tradition.

Some perceptive scholars have noted this dissimulation/decep-
tion component of Santeria and have posed a de facto challenge
to Herskovits' definition of syncretism as it applies to Santeria—the
case of Bastide being a well-known example. Another scholar who
has expounded on this deliberate deception component is Judith
Gleason:

> Once arrived in Cuba, the orishas found it necessary for
> their survival to conceal themselves behind the images
> of certain Catholic saints . . . and certain aspects of Christ

and Our Lady. No matter if the Christian worthies represented by the images had little in common with the
African powers who boldly borrowed their likenesses. A
tower, a sword, the ravages of poverty and disease—one
or two qualities in common, indeed, the most superficial
resemblances were enough. *The Yoruba had found a
coded way* of keeping alive beliefs and rituals that in
other places (where saints were not venerated, nor many
Marias given homage) were suppressed, stamped out,
forgotten. [emphasis added][11]

Sources within the Santeria tradition amply demonstrate the
deliberate nature of dissimulation used by Santeria practitioners. In
a notebook he kept at the beginning of the twentieth century, José
"Bangocheíto" Pérez (1870-1915), a santero, wrote how he advised
one of his followers, a white woman he had initiated to the mysteries
of Obatalá: "Amelia, the white girl from Camaguey who made Obatalá
last May, wants to know if Obatalá is Jesus Nazarene, as they say
over there, or Our Lady of Mercy, as we say here [in Las Villas].
I told her not to worry about the coat, but who wears it."[12] This entry
in Bangocheíto's notebook illustrates that it does not matter by what
Catholic name the orishas are called, as long as those who need to
know are aware of the identity of the orisha being honored behind
the Catholic facade.

My grandmother used to tell the story (possibly apocryphal) of
how in colonial times santeros gave the local church in the town
of Trinidad a huge, costly statue of Saint Barbara. The parish priest
was delighted to receive such a gift for his church and would have
this image carried in parades during feast days. What the parish
priest did not know is that santeros had secretly consecrated the
statue as Shangó, hiding certain implements of the orisha inside it.
When this image of Saint Barbara/Shangó was paraded, followers
of Santeria could worship Shangó publicly without being detected
by the Catholic authorities. Whether this story is true or not is
immaterial. The important element of it is that the identification
of a particular orisha with a particular Catholic saint *within a*

limited geographical area was a conscious and deliberate act, a coded way developed by santeros as a way of fulfilling religious obligations that involved acts of public worship.

As a mnemonic device, in order to facilitate the memorizing of which Catholic saint stood for which orisha, certain superficial similarities between the orisha and the Catholic saint chosen to publicly represent the orisha were noted. Shangó, the warrior king whose emblematic color is red, found an adequate disguise in the girl-martyr Saint Barbara, who is depicted wearing a long red cape, holding a sword, and wearing a crown. Babalú Ayé, the orisha who rules over smallpox, found an analogous Christian image in Lazarus, not the friend of Jesus but the leper in the parable of the rich man and the beggar.

Dissimulation as a device employed by a persecuted people in order to ensure the survival of their religious tradition is a world-wide phenomenon. Ismaili Muslims, faced with opposition from the powerful Sunni branch of Islam, resorted to dissimulation in order to survive. Writes Willi Frischauer in *The Aga Khans:* "Driven underground, they practiced their faith in secret, starting a tradition of secrecy which became second nature to all Ismailis and has survived to this day. Hiding their religious conviction—*taquiya*, which means dissimulation or disguise—became a matter of life and death and permissible as a perfectly honourable practice."[13]

A well-known example of a persecuted people forced into the practice of dissimulation is to be found among the Anusim, or Marrano Jews of Iberia. Beginning in 1391 A.D. these people were coerced into an acceptance of Christianity that in many cases was purely cosmetic, many remaining secretly loyal to Judaism for many years. The case of the Marranos, however, is different from that of Santeria because the great majority of them did, for all practical purposes, eventually lose their original religion, becoming Catholics. A better analogy of the dynamic Santeria/Catholic relationship may be found in Japanese culture, where people tend to practice Shinto and Buddhism interchangeably without either religion losing its individual character and vitality.

Although the original motive behind Santeria's use of Catholic imagery was one of deception in order to achieve survival, it would be wrong to characterize this continuing practice as dishonest. African religious traditions, as well as those of Asia, are generally eclectic and accommodating. The exclusivity one finds in the Judeo-Christian and Islamic faiths is not found in many non-Western traditions.

From a santero's perspective, it is not wrong to celebrate a feast to the orishas on Saturday night and go to mass Sunday morning. Many santeros have developed a genuine affection for Catholic saints and enjoy mass for the same reasons other Catholics do (I say "*other* Catholics" because traditionally, when asked by outsiders to identify their religion, santeros would usually answer, "Catholic"). However, knowledgeable santeros are perfectly aware of the differences between the orishas and the saints. When a santero or santera goes to church, he or she does so as a Catholic. When this same person worships at the feet of the orishas, however, he or she does so in the traditional African manner, with drumming, chanting, and prayers in Lucumí. This has a clear precedent in the context of traditional African religions, where individuals of one tribe can worship another tribe's god without compromising their own god.

Within the complex world of Santeria/Catholic interactions, however, some important elements have become fused. These are not the elements usually listed by scholars, such as the much-stated correspondence between orishas and saints, which from a Santeria perspective is a minor dimension of the religion. Use of Catholic iconography in the covering cloths of the soup tureens that hold the sacred stone representations of the orishas is also relatively unimportant—these are discarded and replaced without ceremony. The importance of certain Catholic rituals, such as baptism and funeral masses, however, is undeniable. Every santero is expected to be baptized a Catholic, and part of the funeral rites for dead santeros includes the saying of nine funeral masses—nine being the emblematic number of Oyá, the orisha who guards the gates of the cemetery. Consecrated holy water figures as an ingredient in many Santeria spells and medicinal potions.

Prominent Miami santero Ernesto Prichardo's views on the

relationship between the African and Catholic elements found in Santeria realistically portray certain dynamics of the religion. According to Prichardo, there are two types of syncretisms found in Santeria, which he labels "visible" and "invisible." Prichardo describes visible syncretism as the deliberate appropriation of Catholic iconography, which has become prevalent in Santeria.

Invisible syncretism, on the other hand, is the result of inexact understanding demonstrated by newcomers to the religion. In his work *Oduduwa Obatala*, coauthored with his wife Lourdes, Prichardo presents the following case as an example of the invisible syncretism that occurs when a newcomer to the religion is consecrated a priest of Santeria:

> A man named Juan has grown up in "X" religion. Health problems bring Juan to Santeria, where he is told that if he becomes a *santero*, his health will improve. After his first year of novitiate, Juan, who is 40, begins to practice Santeria, although he lacks [proper] theoretical foundations.[14]

Prichardo goes on to say that, although Juan is technically a high-level initiate, a Santeria priest, his understanding of the religion is at best modest. Juan will continue to use as his point of reference his former religion, demonstrating an unconscious syncretism that is nothing else but poor understanding of Santeria. Were an anthropologist to use Juan as his or her informant, the information obtained from Juan would not be accurate. Other santeros might also offer the anthropologist a syncretistic picture of Santeria, but this would be a conscious act based on the Santeria tradition of speaking at the level of discourse of the one who knows least. A look at the levels of discourse used by experienced practitioners of Santeria, specifically the way African and Catholic elements are merged, clearly represents deliberate dissimulation, not syncretism.

As early as 1950, William Bascom, the scholar of the Yorubas—along with his Cuban-born wife Berta Montero, a scholar in her own right—came close to uncovering the use of Catholic saints as facades in Santeria: "The fundamental importance of the stones in Cuban Santeria was stressed consistently by informants. While chromolithographs and plaster images of the Catholic saints are prominently displayed in the shrines and houses of the santeros, they are regarded as empty ornaments or decorations, which may be dispensed with."[15]

The higher one goes on the Santeria hierarchy, the less relevant Catholicism is to Santeria. As Bascom correctly reported, Catholic images are discarded when worn and are replaced with better-quality images whenever possible; the fundamental stones that represent the orishas, however, are treated as living entities by santeros. Santeros receive the stones of each orisha once in their lives. These stones are given a great amount of care. When a santera or santero dies, the disposal of the stones is a very important matter—whether a relative or follower will inherit them, or whether they are to be disposed of in some other way, such as throwing them in the river.

Based on what I have stated so far, it is not difficult to envision the different levels of discourse that balance Catholic and African elements of Santeria according to the understanding of those involved. Figure 1 elucidates the interactions between African—specifically Yoruba—and Catholic elements in Santeria. A low level of participation in Santeria, as described in Chapter 4, is correlated with a high degree of Catholic elements and a low degree of African elements; a high level of participation is correlated with a low degree of Catholic elements and a high degree of African elements. When people in a higher level of discourse in what I call "the Santeria syncretism continuum" speak with outsiders or lower level participants, they converse at the level common to both, which is the lower level.

Bascom's example of the saints in a santero's home shows how a high-level Santeria initiate would show the outside world (including those uninvolved with Santeria or involved at a low level) a Catholic facade and hide the more African elements of Santeria. Among santeros and babalaos, however, the Catholic trappings—and even the Spanish words to convey them—fall away. Even the religion itself is no longer referred to as Santeria, but Lucumí.

Figure 1 provides an ideal approximation of the European/ African dynamics that operate at the different levels of the hierarchy. In reality, some high-level initiates operate at a lower level of discourse while some outsiders, such as scholars, can engage in relatively high-level discourse. By "non-African (Catholic) elements," I mean such observable behaviors as attendance to mass, reciting Catholic prayers, and petitioning Catholic saints in the popular Catholic modes. By "African elements," I mean reciting prayers in Lucumí, dancing and drumming as forms of worship, and animal sacrifices done in the African manner.

FIGURE 1: THE SANTERIA SYNCRETISM CONTINUUM[16]

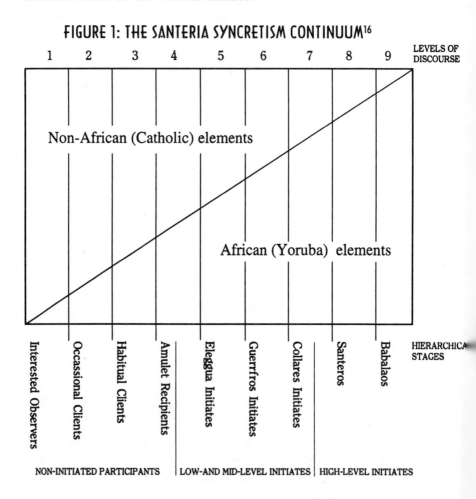

My sources for the construction of this graph include interviews with dozens of people at all levels of the hierarchy; published and unpublished materials written by scholars, low-level initiates, and high-level initiates; and the knowledge provided by my initiation and training as a Santeria priest.

————————————— NOTES —————————————

1. Melville J. Herskovits, *The New World Negro*, edited by Frances S. Herskovits (Bloomington: Indiana University Press, 1966), 322.

2. Herskovits, "African Gods and Catholic Saints in New World, Belief," *American Anthropologist New Series*, XXXIX, no. 4 (1937).

3. Herskovits, *The New World Negro*, 322.

4. Herskovits, "African Gods and Catholic Saints."

5. Joseph M. Murphy, *Santeria: An African Religion in America* (Boston: Beacon Press, 1988), 121.

6. Juan J. Sosa, *La Santeria: A Way of Looking at Reality*, M.A. thesis (Boca Raton, Florida: Florida Atlantic University, 1981), 101.

7. Isidoro Andres Pérez y Mena, *Speaking with the Dead* (New York: AMS Press, 1991), 34.

8. Roger Bastide, *African Religions of Brazil* (Baltimore: Johns Hopkins University Press, 1978), 270.

9. Murphy, 122.

10. Bastide, *African Civilisations in the New World* (New York: Harper Torchbooks, 1971), 156.

11. Judith Gleason, *Santeria: Bronx* (New York: Atheneum, 1975), 206-207.

12. José "Bangocheíto" Pérez, unpublished notebook (c.1911) in Mrs. Haydée Gonzalez's private collection (Havana).

13. Willi Frischauer, *The Aga Khans* (London: Bodley, 1970), 36.

14. L. Ernesto Prichardo and Lourdes Nieto Prichardo, *Oduduwa Obatala* (Miami: St. Babalu Aye Church of the Lucumi, 1984), 26-27.

15. William R. Bascom, "The Focus of Cuban Santeria," *Southwestern Journal of Anthropology*, vol. 6, no. 1 (1950), 65.

16. The blend of Catholic and Yoruba elements typically found at the different levels of discourse corresponding to the different stages of the Santeria hierarchy

CHAPTER 6

SANTERIA'S ORISHAS

Santeria's most popular orishas number less than two dozen, and only a dozen are considered very important. In the complex cosmogony of Santeria, the orishas occupy a vital plane (see Figure 2, page 52). There is a basic, fundamental distinction between orishas who are ritually installed inside priests' or priestesses' heads and those who are not. In the language of Santeria, when a person is said to have "made" *santo*, it means that the person has undergone the kariocha ceremony, where one of the orishas that can be installed has been ritually placed inside that person's head, thus giving the person the right to be called santero or santera.

Traditionally, the seven orishas that can be installed inside a person, the ones that literally define who is a santero or santera, have been called the *Siete Potencias*. Unfortunately most writers have translated *potencia* as power, but are not the orishas other than these seven also powers? Translating *potencia* as power in this case is misleading. *Potencia*, according to definitions one and four, respectively, of the Aristos Spanish dictionary, means " facultad para ejercer una cosa o producir un efecto . . . virtud generativa" (the right to act in a certain capacity or to produce an effect . . . generative strength).[1] The orishas known as the Siete Potencias, then, should be referred to in English as the seven empowering orishas, those that give the santero or santera the generative strength to produce certain effects. In other words, the seven empowering orishas, by virtue of their ability to become a physical part of a santera or santero's being, empower them with the ability to perform certain actions associated with the orishas—such as the power to divine a person's future using cowrie shells—that, without the ashé of these orishas, would be impossible for the santeros to perform.

Obatalá, as head orisha, is the most important of the traditional Siete Potencias. He represents purity and patience. Obatalá has both male and female *caminos* (manifestations). When a person is to be initiated a priest or priestess, not only must he or she find out which orisha is to be installed in his or her head, but which *camino* of the orisha, since most orishas have several manifestations or avatars. Eleggua holds the keys to a person's future and, as messenger of God and the other orishas, can allow or prevent communication between humans and orishas. He is the first orisha to be propitiated in all Santeria ceremonies. Shangó is the lord of thunder and lightning, lord of drumming and dancing, and the epitome of manly beauty. Yemayá is the queen of the oceans, the mother goddess of all orishas. Oshún, queen of rivers, epitomizes female beauty and sensuality; she watches over pregnant women and protects against intestinal disorders. Ogún is the lord of iron and is identified with war. Finally, Oyá rules over storms and lives at the gates of cemeteries.

The powerful orisha Ifá, also called Orula in Cuba, is often included among the Siete Potencias, but the initiatory ceremony for "making ifá" or becoming a babalao, is very different from kariocha. For one thing, Orula is not "seated" in the initiate's head but taken into his very soul. In order for the ifá ceremony to be performed, an extremely sacred artifact representing Olofi (an aspect of God Almighty, Olodumare) must be present. According to Cuban anthropologist Natalia Bolivar Arostegui, this Olofi artifact—probably a sacred, ritually prepared ancient stone—was brought to Cuba in the last part of the nineteenth century. After Cuba freed its slaves in 1880, some decided to go back to Africa. One of these was the legendary santero from Matanzas province, Eulogio Gutierrez. Arriving in Ile-Ife, the Oni, or emperor of Ife, recognized Eulogio as an *oba*— a king—and instructed him to become initiated as a *babalawo* (the term used in Africa), a priest of Ifá. After Gutierrez had lived in Africa happily for ten years, Ifá instructed him through his oracle to return to Cuba and initiate babalaos there. Returning reluctantly to Matanzas with the Olofi artifact, Gutierrez, by now a wealthy man, bought the same sugarcane plantation where he had been a slave and instituted the cult of Ifá among Cuban santeros.

Another Olofi artifact is said to have been smuggled to Cuba by a slave called Villalonga in the 1860s, but he hid his Olofi for many years. Villalonga also created new babalaos—but under very secretive circumstances. As far as is known, these two Olofi artifacts have been used to initiate all babalaos in Cuba. Carlos Ojeda supposedly brought one of these Olofis to Miami in the 1960s, thus bringing the Ifá cult to the United States.

Besides the Siete Potencias and Ifá, other important orishas are Babalú Ayé, lord of leprosy, smallpox, and other skin ailments; Aggayú, lord of volcanoes, closely associated with Shangó; Inle, lord of medicinal herbs; Osain, lord of all plants; Ochosi, the hunter; the Ibeyi, twin child orishas thought to be sons of Shangó; Olokun, powerful androgynous ruler of the ocean depths, closely associated with Yemayá; Orishaoko, lord of agriculture; Dada, older sister or foster mother of Shangó; Yewa, virgin orisha of the cemetery; Nana Burukú, the moon, associated with Babalú Ayé and with snakes;

Obba, Shangó's principal wife; Oddudúa, sometimes identified with Obatalá. These orishas are not usually installed in the heads of Santeria priests and priestesses but are said to be "received" by them—and sometimes by non-santeros as well—in ceremonies particular to each orisha. Whereas the ashé of the Siete Potencias is implanted in a santero's or santera's head, during the initiatory ceremonies of these other orishas their power—represented by a particular artifact—is placed on the initiate's shoulder so that he or she can feel or "receive" the orisha's ashé and protection. However, the ashé does not become fused with the initiate's being, as is the case with the Siete Potencias or Ifá.

Other orishas, considered minor, include Aña, spirit of the batá drums, a servant of Shangó; Ósun, watcher of doors, servant of Eleggua; Iroko, the spirit of the kapok tree; and Oshumare, the rainbow. Other orishas who used to be mentioned in Cuban Santeria notebooks up to the turn of the century but for some reason are no longer generally known include Olosi, orisha of lakes and lagoons; Olosa, guardian of doorways, whose function has been taken over by Eleggua and Ósun; Aroni, lord of dogs; Oggán, Obón, and Ogboni, Obatalá's helpers; Ayaná, a river orisha; Aja, a plant orisha, probably replaced by Inle and Osain; Chugudú, another servant of Eleggua; Ayao, a sister of Oyá; and Boromú, a desert orisha whose cult probably declined because there are no deserts in Cuba.

Figure 2 (page 52) illustrates the realms the orishas occupy and how the orishas relate to one another and to those initiated in Santeria.

1. **Material Plane:** The world of the flesh. In the case of humans (animals and plants are much more a part of both the material and the spiritual worlds), it consists of aleyos, some of whom become santeros, some of whom become babalaos. These stages—aleyo, santero, babalao—determine accessibility to the other planes.

2. **Spiritual Plane:** The world of the spirit; also called world of truth. This is the natural next stage we will all pass to when we leave matter behind, when we die. It is inhabited by beings—

FIGURE 2: SANTERIA COSMOGONY

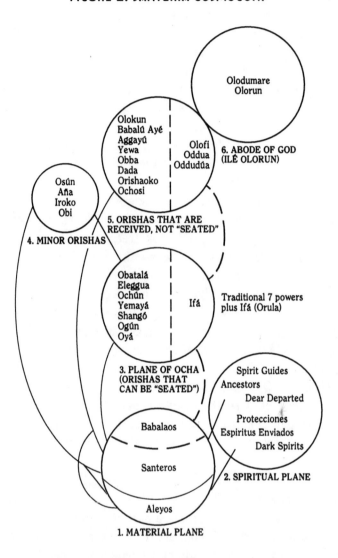

The material plane depicts the levels of direct accessibility. All orishas and planes accessed by aleyos (outsiders) are also accessed by santeros. All orishas and planes accessed by santeros are also accessed by babalaos, though not necessarily by aleyos, as shown by the solid lines. There are, however, some orishas and planes accessed only by babalaos; these are shown by dotted lines.

eres—ranging from *espiritus de gran luz* to *espiritus obscuros*. Beings in this plane are in constant contact with beings in the material world. Everyone can access this plane, even though specialists such as mediums may be more adept at it. Relations between spirits and material beings are complex and reciprocal, spirits helping people as well as hindering them, and people helping spirits can gain light but can also use them for nefarious purposes.

3. Plane of Ocha (orishas that can be "seated"): These are the traditional Siete Potencias, the seven orishas (sometimes classified as *ochas* to distinguish them from those that can't be seated) that are installed in santeros' heads in the kariocha ceremony. These seven—Obatalá, Eleggua, Yemayá, Ochún, Shangó, Ogún, and Oyá—plus Orula (Orunmila, Ifá), who identifies the babalao, are the most important orishas in Santeria, the ones that possess their children (with the exception of Ifá, who doesn't actually possess babalaos) and receive the greatest amount of worship. These are referred to as the orishas that can be "made" (*hacer santo, hacer ocha*).

4. Minor Orishas: Sometimes referred to as nature spirits, these are generally received in conjunction with some aspect of the traditional seven—Ósun along with Ogún and Eleggua in the warriors, for example—and are not the subject of much particular worship or devotion.

5. Orishas That Are Received: Because their ashé is not meant to be contained inside a person's head—either because it is too overwhelming, as in the case of Olokun, or too immature and wild, as in the case of the Ibeyi—these orishas are not made. They are received, either post-kariocha or by aleyos, depending on the circumstances. Sometimes they are received in conjunction with one of the seven—Olokun with Yemayá, for example. These orishas—with the possible exceptions of Babalú Ayé and Aggayú—never possess humans, but songs and dances of praise are performed in their honor. The extremely rare conferring of Olofi and Oddua/Oddudúa is open only to certain babalaos, who then are variously known as *obas* or *olúos*. Although Lydia Cabrera reports there are no Olofi-owning babalaos in the United States, I have it from various sources that the Miami babalao Carlos Ojeda is a bona fide *oba*. Olofi is thought to be the most reachable aspect of God (Olodumare, Olorun).

6. Abode of God (Ilé Olorun): This is where God Almighty resides, alone, with only occasional visits from the only two personages that know where Ilé Olorun is—Obatalá and Eleggua. Olodumare/Olorun is the *deus otioso* (supreme god) of Santeria. He left the world and retired, parceling out much of his ashé to the different orishas, who receive the bulk of devotion and cultic worship in Santeria. God is, however, always mentioned simply because he is God, though for favors and blessings, one deals with the orishas, especially the Siete Potencias.

ELEDÁ

Santeria teaches that, just as everyone has an earthly mother and father, each person also has an orisha mother and father. Moreover, just as children exhibit characteristics inherited from their earthly parents, they also exhibit traits associated with their orisha parents. Orishas are said to possess faults as well as virtues. The orishas' faults, however, are to be interpreted as sacred stories rather than as actual imbalances, for the orishas are thought to be repositories of Olodumare's ashé. These sacred stories, or patakíes, of the supposed frailties of the orishas help humans understand their own character flaws—personality traits that tend to contribute to states of imbalance—thus helping people find remedies for the imbalance these faults may precipitate.

Of the two orisha parents each person has, one asserts him- or herself more strongly on that person's life, becoming such a person's primary spiritual parent. These primary spiritual parents are called eledás. Santeros claim they can usually tell a person's spiritual parent by the way a person looks or acts. A beautiful, flirtatious girl is said to be a daughter of Oshún. Virile men who like to dance and have quick tempers belong to Shangó. Peace-loving, calm, dignified individuals are mostly sons and daughters of Obatalá. Sometimes an orisha's mythic faults are so evident in a person's character— Shangó's violent temper, for example—that in order for that person to regain balance, he or she has to have an infusion of his or her parental orisha's ashé. This is accomplished by having the orisha's ashé installed directly on the person's head in the kariocha ceremony.

When a person agrees to have his or her eledá installed inside his or her head, that person enters into a very serious contract with the orisha. As an *omo* (spiritual child of an orisha), the initiate agrees to keep certain taboos. In exchange, the orisha will give the *omo* peace, tranquility, and health, as well as other benefits. The taboos the *omo* must keep usually involve dietary restrictions such as not eating foods sacred to the orisha and avoiding certain places or situations. The *omo* who agrees to undergo initiation also agrees to perform certain rituals periodically. The eledá protects the *omo* from undeserved harm, but the orisha may not have to protect the *omo* from all harm, since all are expected to pay for their imbalance-causing actions.

ITÁ

"You Cubans are crazy," my Nigerian friend tells me. "You have bastardized my religion! Where did you get the idea that Iemonja (Yemayá) and Osún (Oshún) are blood sisters? And saying that Orunmila (Orula) is Sango's (Shangó's) younger brother is utter nonsense! Don't you realize that Orunmila was present when the world was made, while Sango is a deified king, a historical figure, the fourth *alafin* (king) of Oyo? Who can understand you people!"

Itá is Lucumí hagiography, the life and times of the orishas. Devotees of Santeria believe these myths hold eternal truths and valuable lessons and they have passed them on from one gereration to another for hundreds—in some cases possibly thousands—of years. Although the orishas in Santeria are the same as those in the Yoruba pantheon, their stories are markedly different in Cuba. The greatest difference between the African and Cuban patakíes, or stories, is that, in Cuba, all of the orishas are said to be blood-related. Because this familial relationship was superimposed on the African deities in relatively recent times and in different parts of Cuba, there is a great deal of contradiction from ilé to ilé as to just how one orisha is related to another. Some of the liveliest arguments among santeros involve such discussions as to whether Shangó is the son or brother of Aggayú. Each ilé holds its interpretation to be the correct one.

Interestingly, all ilés agree that it is important to understand the orishas as members of a single family. This imposition of family ties on orishas who in Africa were very distant, in some cases totally independent of one another, may in fact be a reflection of the different Yoruba-speaking peoples who were brought forcibly to Cuba and who united under a single name, Lucumí. The Lucumí "nation" in Cuba included people from different areas who in Africa had been distinct groups, even enemies. Realizing the need to unite against a common oppressor, all these different Yoruba-speaking peoples began to see themselves as a single nation, their varied cults as a single religion, and their deities as part of one pantheon.

For the following patakíes, which represent only a miniscule part of the rich Lucumí trove of myths, I draw upon stories told to me by Amanda, by Juan García and his then-centenarian mother, and by Paco Cuevas; I also use myths written down in notebooks that friends and relatives have allowed me to copy and translate. I have tried to relate myths that are most familiar and that, in many cases, are to be found in some form in such reliable texts as those of Lydia Cabrera. It is important to remember that these myths represent the interpretation of ilés I have been associated with. On reading these myths many santeros—I can almost hear them—will say: "No, he's got it wrong, that's not the way that story goes!" Their opinions are valid, but to put down all the existing versions of each myth would prove an exhausting task well beyond the scope of this work.

Genesis

In the beginning was Ashé and Ashé was everything. When Ashé began to think, Ashé became Olodumare. When Olodumare began to act, Olodumare became Olofi, and it was Olofi who created Obatalá, the first orisha. In those days there was no separation between heaven and earth, and Olodumare used to come down to earth very often. In one of his visits, Olofi fashioned humankind out of mud, but he left the people without heads, wandering aimlessly. It was Obatalá who finished Olofi's work, giving humankind heads, which is the reason that to this day Obatalá is the owner of everyone's head. In order to bring fertility to the world, Obatalá became two beings, one male, one female. The male Obatalá called himself Oddudúa; the female called herself Yemmu. The first four children of Oddudúa and Yemmu were Olokun, the sea, an androgynous deity of immense power; Aggayú, the mountains and volcanoes, ruler of the sun; Orishaoko, the harvest; and Babalú Ayé, the swamp, lord of disease. These four orishas are extremely powerful; they have almost as much ashé as Obatalá.

The Incest

Obatalá-Oddudúa was worried about the amount of attention his wife, Obatalá-Yemmu, was bestowing on their son Ogún, lord of iron. Yemmu treated her son not as a mother would but as a woman in love. Oddudúa had an enchanted rooster, Ósun, who was supposed to inform him of all that went on in the house while Oddudúa was away. So far, Ósun had not reported any unusual behavior between Ogún and his mother. After some time Oddudúa noticed that his son Eleggua, the eternal child, was sullen and emaciated. "What is wrong, Eleggua?" asked Oddudúa. "Why are you so sad?"

"Baba-mi," answered Eleggua, "I hurt to have to tell you, but Ogún has been doing a horrible deed with Mother; he gives all my food to Ósun so that Ósun goes to sleep and then he locks me out of the house so that I don't see what goes on, but I know."

That night, Oddudúa told Yemmu to prepare him some food to last a couple of days, for he would be going away. No sooner had Oddudúa left on his supposed journey than Ogún and Yemmu began to make love. Oddudúa, who had not gone very far, came back and surprised his wife and son in the shameful act. Covering his face in horror, Ogún cried, "Do not curse me, Baba-mi, for I curse myself. For the rest of my life I shall not cease to work, laboring day and night. No longer will I know the peace of rest. I will teach mankind the secret of making iron, so that not even lord of iron will I be."

"And so it shall be," declared Oddudúa. "Go now, and never return." Turning to Yemmu, Oddudúa said, "You I cannot curse, for I would be cursing myself, but the next man-child you have, I'll bury alive." Looking at his beloved baby boy Shangó, Oddudúa said, "Shangó will go live with his sister Dada on top of the palm tree, only Eleggua will stay by my side." Turning to Ósun, Oddudúa said: "From this day on you will eat only what Eleggua chooses to throw at you, and forever you will serve him."

Orula

Shortly after Ogún was banished from Oddudúa's house, Yemmu became pregnant. When a baby boy was born, Oddudúa ordered Yemmu to bury him alive. Heartbroken, Yemmu buried the child from the neck down at the foot of the sacred Iroko tree. Yemmu knew that Iroko would care for her child, whom she named Orula. From Iroko, Orula learned the secrets of divination. At the foot of the tree, buried from the neck down, Orula became the greatest of all diviners, the *baba l'awo*, or father of the mysteries. People would come to Orula and give him food in exchange for having their fortunes told. Orula's fame grew and one day Eleggua came to see him, recognizing his brother. "Don't worry, Orula," said Eleggua, "I'll ask Father to forgive you."

For a long time Eleggua used his most persuasive arguments to make Oddudúa forgive his son Orula. Finally, the old orisha went to see Orula. Oddudúa cried when he saw the young man buried from the neck down. Lifting his arm, Oddudúa ordered the earth to release Orula. "Come, my son, we are going home."

Startled, Orula said, "I beg my father's forgiveness, but I cannot leave the shadow of Iroko, for he has been like a mother to me."

Looking at the tree-god, Oddudúa said, "Do not worry, Orula, for

Iroko will always be with you." Pointing to the tree, Oddudúa released a ray of energy that turned it into a round tray, which Orula lovingly took with him. It is in this tray that Orula—and his spiritual descendants, the babalaos—cast fortunes.

Because of what Eleggua did for him, Orula became very close to his brother. Old santeros say that only babalaos, the priests of Orula, have the ashé necessary to confer the Eleggua—and the guerreros—initiation.

SHANGÓ

The most popular orisha in Santeria is Shangó, lord of thunder. No other orisha has so many myths attached to him. Shangó was probably a historical figure, the fourth king of the Yorubas and third *alafin* (king) of the city-state of Oyo. As the Shangó myth grew, he was syncretized with a much older deity, Jakuta, and inherited much of the legends attached to Jakuta. One of the most sacred secrets of Santeria, revealed only to a select few, is that Shangó is the only orisha who ever tasted death. Santeros become extremely nervous when speaking of the so-called *obakoso* (king did not hang himself) incident. There are several myths about the birth of Shangó. The one I have already told makes him a son of Oddudúa and Yemmu; another myth makes Aggayú his father and Yemayá his mother. Still another myth tells how Olofi sent Shangó to earth as a baby in a ball of fire, with Yemayá adopting him and raising him as her own. Amanda used to say "Obatalá Yemmu is his mother, but Yemayá raised him as her own when Oddudúa ordered him out." Following are a few of the hundreds of Shangó myths.

Shangó's Enmity with Ogún

Although Oddudúa banished Shangó to Dada's house in order to prevent mother-son incest from occurring again in his household, the father was very fond of his beautiful baby boy. Oddudúa had Shangó brought to him almost every day. When Shangó was a strapping young man, Oddudúa told him the story of Ogún's incest with Yemmu. Filled with hatred for his brother, Shangó swore to avenge his father. "Baba, who is Ogún's wife?"

"Oyá, queen of the storms and of the gates of the cemetery."

"I shall steal Ogún's wife so that he suffers what you suffer, my father," said Shangó.

Fully attired in his regal robes, Shangó mounted his magnificent stallion Echinlá and went to look for Oyá. The courageous and beautiful queen of the storms could not resist Shangó, the most perfect example of male beauty. She left the homely Ogún, never to return to him. Since that day, Shangó and Ogún have been mortal enemies. This is why when one santero becomes possessed by Ogún and another by Shangó, they must be kept apart so that they do not kill each other's *caballo* (medium).

Shangó's Three Women

Shangó's legitimate wife is Obba, dignified queen of his castle. However, no one woman can satisfy the god of virility; Shangó needs the fire and passion that his two main mistresses, Oyá and Oshún, bring to him. Obba offers Shangó undying devotion and stability, for she is the patron orisha of homemakers. Oshún, the Yoruba Aphrodite, gives Shangó the sensual pleasures he craves, while Oyá—probably his favorite—is the only woman he takes to war; she is as good a warrior as he is.

Obba's Ear

Obba, the dignified wife of Shangó, wanted to arouse in her husband the same kind of passion his mistress Oshún did. Pretending to feel sorry for Obba, the devious Oshún told Obba to cut off one of her own ears and serve it to Shangó in his favorite dish, *amala,* made with cornmeal and okra. Wanting more than anything to please her husband, Obba did as she was told. When Shangó came home that evening, after he ate his amala he noticed that Obba was wearing a bandage over one ear. When he learned what was wrong with her, Shangó was enraged and repulsed and in a loud voice told Obba, "I swear by my father that I'll never sleep with you again! What you have done to me is disgusting! You will always be my wife and the mistress of my castle, but I'll never lie with you again."

Since that day Obba has become a symbol of wifely abnegation and devotion. She rarely possesses her devotees, but they like to dance a slow, dignified dance for her, which is done with one hand covering the right ear, as a memorial to her sacrifice.

Why Shangó Fears the Dead

One of the characteristics that identifies the devotees of Shangó is their fear of the dead. This is unique in Santeria, a religion that places enormous importance on propitiating the dead. "No hay santo sin muerto" (There's no orisha without the spirits of the dead) is a Santeria proverb. All ceremonies in Santeria begin with a prayer to the dead, and in all Santeria rituals the ancestors and guardian spirits are propitiated first. As the story goes Shangó, then known as Jakuta in Ile-Ife, the holy city of the orishas, wanted more than anything to experience life as a human. Shangó descended to the city of Oyo, becoming its alafin (king). In this manifestation Shangó is called Alafin and is greeted with the phrase "Cabio sile" (Welcome, lord).

As a human king Shangó was not very successful; he should have never left Ile-Ife. Because his subjects were always complaining and his three women did not take well to human life, Shangó felt constant strain. One night, not being able to take it any longer, in a characteristic burst of anger Shangó went to the forest and hung himself on a cedar tree. Some of his subjects saw his body and began to spread the rumor, "Oba so," the king had hung himself. Shangó, an orisha, found himself in the world of the *iku*, the dead, an experience he was never to forget and one that would forever haunt him. After seven days, Obatalá found out what had happened and rescued his son from the dead, returning his immortality to him. From Ile-Ife, Shangó could see his former subjects in Oyo laughing at him, saying, "Oba so! Oba so!" Using his power over lightning, Shangó struck dead each person who said "Oba so!" Since that day, any time it thunders the people of Oyo say "oba ko so"—(the king did not hang himself). This story is one seldom told in Santeria, for Shangó is thought not to like stories of his ordeal as a human—and as a dead person—being recounted. Many santeros today ignore the meaning of the phrase "obakoso." Even Lydia Cabrera errone-ously translates "obakoso" as "king of Koso." As one informant told

Cabrera when she tried to find out the story of Shangó's death, "There are things in Santeria one cannot talk about, and the matter of Shangó's rest is one of them." "Shangó's rest" is a euphemism used in Santeria for his death.

Shangó Trades Gifts with Orula

Shangó was born with the gift of divining. He could tell a person's future just by looking at that person. Orula, on the other hand, was the best dancer and drummer in the world but did not think much of these gifts since his passion was to become the best diviner in the universe. Although Orula spent years carefully studying all kinds of divination, he could never be as great a diviner as Shangó. Shangó, on the other hand, wished he had Orula's musical gifts, for although the beautiful thunder-god tried, his dancing was less than graceful and his drumming only average.

One day at a party, after Shangó enviously watched Orula dance, the thunder god told his brother, "I would gladly trade my powers of divination for your musical gifts, Orula." Orula could not believe his ears: would Shangó seriously consider giving him the greatest of gifts in exchange for such frivolities?

Not wanting to take advantage of Shangó, Orula warned him, "You should think carefully before you speak, brother, you are offering to give up the greatest of gifts."

"That is not true, Orula. Your grace on the dance floor and your dexterity on the drums are the greatest of gifts; if I could get them, I would truly feel the most perfect of beings."

"Let us not talk about it anymore, then," said Orula. "Let us embrace and will our gifts on each other."

After the orishas exchanged gifts, Shangó became a better dancer and drummer than Orula ever had been, while Orula's powers of divination gave him so much status that some say he is Obatalá's equal in power. Neither orisha ever regretted his decision, each maintaining he got the best part of the deal.

THE GREAT FLOOD AND WHY PEOPLE DROWN

Back when there were only six orishas in Ile-Ife, the androgynous deity of the sea, Olokun, dared to challenge Obatalá's supremacy over orishas and humans alike. Olokun was enormously powerful; Olofi had made the mistake of bestowing too much power on the ruler of the seas. To show Obatalá his or her power, Olokun made the waters rise, totally covering the earth and killing everything except the orishas and the few animals and humans who were able to hang on to a silver ladder Obatalá sent down from Ilé Olorun, the heavens, where all orishas had gone to seek refuge. Not even Obatalá could contain Olokun by himself, but Olodumare, who had earlier made a vow never to interfere in worldly affairs again, made an exception and increased Obatalá's awesome power.

Obatalá—with the help of Olodumare himself—tied Olokun down with seven huge silver chains. Olokun gave up but asked Obatalá to give him one human life per day, to which Obatalá agreed. This is why people drown and why, in Cuba, the descendants of the Lucumí are never sailors. This story also teaches not to take God Almighty for granted, for although he is removed, one never knows when he might be needed.

Why God Left the World

In the beginning, Olofi, the orishas, and the humans all lived in harmony. Soon, however, the orishas began to demand more and more ashé from God. Some even plotted against him; only Eleggua remained totally faithful. Even Obatalá, who was part of God himself, sometimes defended his beloved humans to the point of taking their side against God. Once when he picked up a human baby, Olofi was splashed with diarrhea, which disgusted the impeccable god. What really made Olofi leave the earth, however, was that he had become so identified with the earth that every time a root was pulled to be cooked, he felt as if his hair was being pulled out by the roots. Fed up, Olofi left the earth, creating a chasm between his abode and the world; only Obatalá and Eleggua know how to reach him. Olofi deserves veneration because he is God, but one should not ask him for favors; that is why he left the orishas behind, to take care of human needs.

How Disease Entered the World

At a great feast given by Obatalá in Ile-Ife, all of the orishas danced and sang. The powerful Shopona, who was lame, also danced. Because of his handicap Shopona looked awkward in some of the fast dances, and some of the orishas laughed at him. He was so overcome with anger at this that he unleashed all manner of plagues on the entire world. Obatalá just barely contained disease among the orishas but was unable to contain it among humans, and he banished Shopona from Ile-Ife. Shopona moved to the land of Arará, where he became the beloved Babalú Ayé, the Father of the World. From Arará, regretting what he had done, Babalú Ayé dedicated himself to the task of curing people of the plagues he had unleashed in a moment of anger. This story teaches that we should not laugh at handicapped people.

In Africa, Babalú Ayé is considered the god of smallpox and is worshiped out of fear. In Santeria, Babalú Ayé is loved as a father figure and is considered kind and loving. Either Christian influences softened Shopona's character in the New World, or the gentler image of Babalú Ayé is reflective of earlier African conceptions of the orisha.

The Story of Obi

One of Obatalá's children, the prince Obi, lived in a beautiful, resplendent castle high up in the palm trees. There he held court dressed in impeccable white robes of exquisite beauty. Obatalá had installed Obi as the patron orisha of a prosperous region. Obi's court became the most opulent in the world, and kings from throughout the world came to Obi to pay him respect.

Obi's brother, the unpredictable Eleggua, noticed that the young prince had become proud and snobbish. He would neglect his poor and disadvantaged subjects and only receive the rich and powerful in his castle. At one feast given by Obi, only the richest kings were invited. Disguised as a pauper, Eleggua was denied admittance to his brother's castle: "How dare you try to come in in such ragged clothes!" Obi screamed at him, not recognizing Eleggua. "Guards! Take this man away!"

Eleggua ran to Obatalá and told him what had happened. Obatalá also disguised himself as a beggar and, together with Eleggua, went to Obi's castle. "What is this?" cried Obi, indignant. "Another lowlife? To the dungeons with these two!"

"I think you are mistaken, Obi."

Prince Obi immediately recognized the powerful voice of his father and, falling on his knees, covered his face with his hands. He said, "Forgive me, Father, I did not know what I was doing." When Obi took his hands away from his eyes, he saw Obatalá in his radiant form as the "King of the White Cloth."

Raising his hand, Obatalá cursed Obi: "From this day forward, those white clothes you so proudly wear will be inside of you, and you will always wear filthy brown rags on the outside; you will fall down from this palm over and over and children will kick you for sport; your brother orishas and human diviners will cut you in pieces and you will be the simplest of oracles, no longer worshiped, but used." This is the story of how the coconut came into being. Even today, knowledgeable santeros feel great respect for the coconut, for they know of Obi's past glory and his former status as an orisha.

How Oshún Became the Patroness of Cuba[2]

This is one of the few myths told in Santeria that does not have an African origin. This story is obviously a Cuban invention of relatively recent times.

Oshún, goddess of love and of the rivers, watched sadly as great numbers of her children were forcibly taken away to a far-away land called Cuba. Confused about the situation and her inability to stop strange white men from abducting her followers, Oshún went to see her older sister, Mother Yemayá, to ask her advice. "Wise sister, what is happening? Why can't I stop this tragedy from occurring?"

"It had to happen this way, Oshún," answered Yemayá sadly. "Our children will tell the entire world of our wonders, and millions who have forgotten us will worship us again."

Moved by an intense desire to be with her suffering children, Oshún decided on an impulse to move to Cuba. But she had never before left her kingdom, the Oshún River, and was afraid. "Tell me,

Yemayá, you whose seven seas caress all of the lands of the world, what is Cuba like?"

Thinking pensively for a moment, the stately queen answered, "It is much like here: hot days, long nights, lush vegetation, tranquil rivers."

"Is there anything about Cuba and its people I should know before I move there?"

"Yes," answered Yemayá. "Not everyone is black like us; there are also many whites."

Impulsive as she is, Oshún asked Yemayá to grant her two wishes: "Make my hair straighter and my skin lighter so that all Cubans can see a bit of themselves in me."

With a majestic sweep of her hand, Yemayá granted her sister's wishes. That is why Oshún in Cuba has long, wavy hair and light skin; this is why all Cubans worship "Cachita" (the pet name for Oshún), regardless of the color of their skin.

ORACLES

Although some Yoruba scholars have attempted to equate the oracle of Ifá with the Judeo-Christian scriptures, [3] I propose that this is not a valid comparison. The oracle of Ifá consists of a body of sacred stories (patakíes) that a babalao memorizes.[4] By casting a small chain with eight concave oval or round pieces of leather, coconut, or calabash rind attached to it, the babalao obtains a configuration that indicates which *oddu,* or chapter, of the oracle of Ifá is to be recited at a particular moment for a particular inquirer. These stories are usually very ambiguous; the babalao must rely on his ashé to find the correct application of the story to the situation. Although considered highly reliable, the oracle of Ifá is not sought as often as the caracoles or mediloggun oracle. *Caracoles,* or cowrie shells, are said to be the mouths of the orishas. Any Santeria priest or priestess has a right to learn to cast them.

The caracoles oracle is much simpler than the Ifá system. While as many as 256 *oddus* appear in Ifá, only 16 *letras* (equivalent of *oddus*) are evident in caracoles divination. Sixteen cowrie shells are cast; the number of shells that fall with the natural opening facing up determines which *letra* is to be recited. *Letras* one through twelve can be interpreted by any santero or santera; thirteen through sixteen should only be read by babalaos. By far the most frequently consulted oracle in Santeria is the *obi* or coconut-casting system. Anyone can learn to cast coconuts, even the uninitiated. Four pieces of coconut are cast in the *obi* divination system. Depending on the number of pieces that fall with the white pulpy side facing up, a total of five possible answers emerge, including "yes," "no," "maybe," and "consult a more complex oracle." Questions should be formulated in a manner that calls for a "yes" or "no" answer. Some people are very proficient at coconut casting—"they have a lot of ashé"— and can extract a surprising number of answers from this simple oracle.

NOTES

1. *Diccionario de la lengua Española* (Madrid: Aristos, 1980).

2. A version of this myth appears in Mercedes Cros Sandoval, *La religion afrocubana* (Madrid: Playor, 1975), 11-12.

3. See Samuel O. Abogurin, "Ethics in Yoruba Religious Tradition," *World Religions and Global Ethics,* S. Cromwell Crawford, editor (New York: Paragon House, 1989).

4. Anthropologists Judith Gleason and William Bascom have each written English translations of the oracle of Ifá: Judith Gleason, *A Recitation of Ifá* (New York: Grossman, 1973); and William Bascom, *Ifa Divination: Communication Between Gods and Men in West Africa* (Bloomington: Indiana University Press, 1969).

CHAPTER 7

ORO:
DIVINE MUSIC

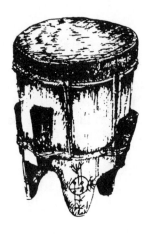

According to practitioners of Santeria, the orishas were able to cross the waters from Africa in the songs of their devotees. Slavemasters deprived their victims of nearly everything, but they could not take from the Lucumí—as the Yoruba people who were brought to Cuba are known—the keys they possessed to gain access to the divine. These keys were held in the melodies produced in their throats and in the complex rhythms of their hands. According to Santeria tradition, highly trained singers and drummers, especially batá drummers, hold the secret ability to create a confluence of sounds and rhythms that bridges the seen and the unseen, the material and the spiritual, God and humankind.[1]

When properly consecrated batá drums, played by initiated drummers called alañas, unite with the sound of faithfully executed vocal melodies and phrases, the orishas descend from their heavenly abode and temporarily possess their devotees, thus initiating a mystic state of communion between the orishas and the participants. Each of these songs must be executed in the exact manner prescribed to achieve the desired effect. A missed beat or a mispronounced word, and the orishas do not come.

One way of explaining the orishas in Western terms—one I'm not particularly fond of but which has received widespread attention—is to equate the orishas with Jungian archetypes. The Jungian archetype is a prototypic phenomenon that simultaneously forms part of the so-called collective unconscious and is accessible to each individual's unconscious. Since these archetypes are believed to reflect human thoughts regardless of place, time, or culture, proponents of equating the orishas with these archetypes argue that in this manner non-Africans may gain an understanding of the orishas. Sacred batá drumming and singing, then, becomes the tool where these archetypes can be glimpsed by the conscious mind.

African theologian John Mbiti has said, "African music is that aspect of life which provides the repositories of traditional beliefs, ideas, wisdom, and feelings."[2] This is true for Santeria music, through which the ancient wisdom of the Yorubas has been passed down to their Lucumí descendants in Cuba. Santeria drumming is almost entirely based on Yoruba patterns.

Since Santeria songs are Yoruba songs that have been preserved in Cuba over hundreds of years, a case can be made that these songs reflect an earlier development in Yoruba music than that which is evident in African Yoruba drumming today. Santeria has preserved ritual African music with remarkable fidelity—no musical activity in Santeria is devoid of the Yoruba worldview.

Although simple cylindrical single drums and so-called conga drums are sometimes used in Santeria to praise the orishas, for the really important ceremonies only the consecrated, fundamental batá drums are used. The batá are two-toned drums particular to the Yoruba people of West Africa and their New World descendants, especially the Lucumí of Cuba and the Nago of Brazil. The batá drum has a mahogany body in the shape of a truncated cone—drums made in Cuba are shaped somewhat like asymmetrical hourglasses—with two heads of different size and tone. The heads are covered with goatskins laced together with leather strips. These are then wrapped tightly against the body of the drum with other leather strips, which tune them tightly and produce a fixed tone. Small cast bells are attached to the leather strips. Three drums make up the batá ensemble. In Cuba, the largest drum is called the Iyá, the middle one the Itótele, and the smallest one the Okónkolo—in Africa, they are known as Iyá Ilú, Omele, and Kudi.

Musically speaking, Santeria batá drumming is considered one of the hardest and most complex forms to learn. One of its notable rhythmic features is the sometimes contrasting tempos each of the three drums keeps. Each of the six hands involved in the batá ensemble plays a particular phrase; all of these phrases combine to form a polyrhythmic single phrase, a symphonic synthesis of rhythms, tonalities, and chords. The batá drums are said to be able to "speak"; Iyá and Itótele usually carry on a complex conversation, while Okónkolo maintains a basic rhythm. Santeros consider properly consecrated batá drums to be living, powerful entities, the materialization of the great spirit Aña.

To properly consecrate the batá drums, three very complex ceremonies must be carried out. The first takes place during the construction of the bodies of the drums; the second is held right before the goat hides are affixed to them; and the third, sometimes called the "blessing of the drums," is performed after the drums have been built but before they are played for the first time. To make a batá drum set, a highly trained artisan especially ordained to this function chooses three pieces of mahogany with the help of an oracle. Once the three pieces have been chosen, Osain, the orisha who rules over plants, must be propitiated and his blessing sought. The three pieces of wood are then washed in omiero, a sacred herbal infusion that begins the process of imbuing the drums with supernatural power. The spirit called Aña is then honored with an animal sacrifice, usually a rooster. He is then consulted using the coconut oracle to determine whether the sacrifice was satisfactory.

For the second ceremony three babalaos are needed, as well as an alaña (consecrated drummer who owns a batá set himself), an oriaté (senior priest), and the future alaña (the person for whom the drums are being built). After they are gathered, more omiero is poured on the drums-in-construction while the blessings of the orishas known as warriors—Eleggua, Ogún, Ochosi, and Ósun—are sought. Next the Ibeyi, Shangó, Obatalá, and again Osain are invoked. Any negative response on the part of the orishas being consulted will result in the whole operation being cancelled. Assuming that all these orishas give their blessings, the three babalaos then consult the Ifá oracle to find out the *oddu,* or sacred prophetic verse, that characterizes each of the drums, as well as the collective name by which the set of three will be known. At this time, it is also customary to ask what animal or animals should be sacrificed to the individual spirit who will possess each of the drums. These spirits are thought to reside in small iron cauldrons that were prepared with magical implements for this purpose. The sacrifices are offered to the cauldrons as well as to the drums themselves. The established alaña takes some of the ingredients from his own cauldrons and places them in the cauldrons of the set being built, thus imbuing them with power. The cauldrons then receive a collective name. The drums are believed to speak to their owner through the magic cauldrons.

The next stage in the construction of the batá set focuses on affixing the goatskins to the drum bodies. A specially prepared kola nut known as an implin is affixed to the first strap of each drum. The Iyá drum, the biggest, is prepared first. Inside the goatskin of the smaller head, the *oddus* and other signs are written with chalk or red paint. The *afoubo,* or so-called secret, a small leather bag containing parrot feathers, two large glass beads, and other ingredients, is then placed inside the Iyá drum. Aña is thought to reside in the afoubo. The bag is then nailed to the inside of the body of the drum. After the Iyá has been prepared, the Itótele and the

Okónkolo follow. Next, more animals are sacrificed. This time, the men can cook and partake of the flesh of the sacrificed animals (traditionally, women do not participate in batá consecration ceremonies). The final sacrifice usually consists of three white roosters, three cornish hens, three brown hens, three white doves, three black doves, one turtle, one *jutía* (a Cuban rodent about the size and appearance of an opossum), three waterfowl, smoked fish, palm oil, and grated coconut. The goatskins are secured to the three drums.

The third ceremony enhances the new drums' ashé. The elder drummers first begin to play their own batás; they then give their drums to the neophyte drummer to play while they play the newly consecrated set so that they can share their ashé with the new drums. The new alaña then returns the elder drummers' batás to them and they in turn give the newly consecrated set to the new alaña, who now plays his properly prepared sacred instruments for the first time.

As can be seen even in this perfunctory account of how a batá set is made, an enormous amount of psychic energy goes into its manufacture. It is little wonder, then, that santeros consider the sounds made by such drums to be magical.

The ability of African and African American drumming to access feelings that are often untapped in Western societies is beginning to be acknowledged. Dr. John Bolling, a noted psychiatrist in New York City, recognizes the therapeutic value of African drumming. He believes that traditional Western psychiatry is missing an important spiritual element. In his pioneering work with African American youths in Harlem, Dr. Bolling makes use of African music, particularly drumming, as part of his therapy; he says, "Music and drumming, especially drumming, synchronizes the soul and its different levels of energy."[3] Afro-Cubans have been deriving therapeutic value from Santeria drumming for hundreds of years.

I have attended hundreds of bembés in Cuba, New York, Puerto Rico, California, Miami, and Tampa. I have often taken guests who are unfamiliar with the Santeria tradition—in some cases people who had never before heard African drumming. Generally, the comment

I hear from these people after they have been exposed to the music is that they have experienced an inexplicable outpouring of energy similar to the power of an erupting volcano.[4] I have no doubt that preserving these powerful songs has contributed to the unique, proud character of the Afro-Cuban ethos, a pride often expressed in the ability to maintain their traditions under very difficult circumstances.

NOTES

1. For a thorough study of Santeria drumming and its importance to the religion, see Robert Alan Friedman, *Making an Abstract World Concrete* (Ann Arbor: University Microfilms, 1982).

2. John Mbiti, *African Religions and Philosophy* (New York: Doubleday, 1970), 87.

3. "Secret African City," BBC television documentary, 1988.

4. The audiocassette *Sacred Sounds of Santeria* (Rochester, Vermont: Destiny Recordings, 1992) contains a selection of Santeria drumming and songs.

CHAPTER 8

SANTERIA AND ESPIRITISMO

Espiritismo, or Spiritism, is indispensable to modern Cuban Santeria. *Spiritism* refers to Kardecian teachings, especially as practiced in Latin America, while *spiritualism* refers to the nineteenth-century mediumistic movement in the United States. In the Brazilian religion Umbanda, spiritism has been clothed with African concepts, resulting in a tradition that has been termed *Afro-Spiritist.*[1] Santeria does not blend spiritist concepts into its ethos in the same way Umbanda does, but it nevertheless depends on spiritist practices in order to fulfill certain obligations to the deceased members of the community. Although Spiritism serves a valuable function in Santeria, it has not been absorbed by it. A saying in Cuba goes, "All santeros are Spiritists, but not all Spiritists are santeros." This is true to a large degree, for Santeria has come to depend on certain spiritist practices, but Spiritism—specifically the Kardecian kind—has retained its own identity and non-African character.

Allan Kardec, the founder of Kardecism, was born Hypolite Léon Denizard Rivail on October 3, 1804, in Lyons, France.[2] A highly regarded teacher with a solid academic background, Rivail published eight scholarly books between 1824 and 1849. At the age of fifty-one, after having established his academic reputation, Rivail came in contact with Spiritism.

Spiritualism had swept across North America in the middle of the nineteenth century. In the years 1854 and 1855, mediumistic phenomena invaded Europe from the United States; at this time Rivail, who had a keen interest in paranormal phenomena, was introduced to turning table and talking table séances. Convinced of the authenticity of such phenomena, Rivail began to see himself as appointed by the spirits to codify Spiritism. He adopted the name of a previous incarnation, a druid from ancient Gaul named Allan Kardec.

Kardec turned his considerable talents to writing about Spiritism, developing a comprehensive philosophy in such works as *Qu'est-ce-que le Spiritisme?* [What is Spiritism?] (1859); *Le Livre des mediums* [The Book of Mediums] (1861); and *L'Evangile selon de spiritisme* [The Message of Spiritism] (1864). *The Encyclopedia of Religion* provides a succinct description of the Kardecian spiritist doctrine:

> There are souls, or spirits, of deceased persons that are capable of communication with the living through mediumistic phenomena. They belong to an invisible but natural world; there is no discussion of magic, miracles, and the supernatural in Kardecism. This invisible and non-material world is, as part of the natural world, susceptible to experimentation, but, unlike the natural world, it is eternal and preexistent and is identified with goodness, purity and wisdom. There is a spiritual hierarchy

ranging from that most identified with the material plane (and hence with evil, impurity, and ignorance) up to that of spiritual fullness.

God is the primary cause that generates the material and the spiritual; the spirits are engendered by him, and although they receive a mission and submit to the law of constant progress, they are endowed with free will. Spirits continually progress toward perfection, and they fulfill their mission through successive reincarnations, not only on earth (considered a planet of atonement) but also on other worlds. The law of cause and effect explains human happiness or misfortune as consequences of good or evil practiced in previous incarnations. Christian charity is the supreme virtue (Christ is considered the most elevated spirit that has ever incarnated) that makes spiritual evolution possible; it is closely followed in importance by the virtue of wisdom. As the locus of the activity of the developing but morally free spirits and as the product of evolution, the social world, even with its injustices and inequalities, is seen as ultimately just, and the search for perfection is ruled by individualistic ethics.[3]

Kardecism rapidly spread to Latin America, acquiring great popularity in Cuba and Brazil. In Brazil Kardecism permeated the entire culture—there is even a Brazilian postage stamp with Kardec's picture on it. Although the Catholic Church condemned Kardec's books, Kardecian séances were the rage in nineteenth-century Havana and other Cuban cities and became the favorite parlor game of the upper classes.

The growth of Kardecism among the well-to-do coincided with the decline of the Yoruba/Lucumí *egungun* specialists in Cuban Santería. The egungun were highly trained specialists in the Lucumí tradition whose presence at funerals was deemed indispensable. They had the ability to become possessed by the spirit of the departed, a necessary part of Lucumí funeral rituals. Apparently, not many egungun were brought to Cuba, and few Cuban-born blacks learned the ways of the egungun. By the middle of the nineteenth century, the egungun was a dying institution in Cuba. As Lydia Cabrera has pointed out, if the egungun rituals were not carried out exactly according to tradition, the person attempting to perform the ritual would fall down dead.[4] It is hardly surprising that few chose to risk their lives by learning the ways of the egungun.

The demise of the egungun must have caused some consternation in late nineteenth-century Cuban Santeria, for a practice deemed essential in the all-important cult of the ancestors was becoming extinct. About this time, Lucumí house servants began to notice that their masters—or more often their masters' wives—were becoming possessed of the spirits of their own ancestors through a practice called *Espiritismo*. The house servants also observed that the white people were doing this without much risk to their lives. With the wonderful adaptability that characterizes Afro-Cuban culture, santeros appropriated the technical, mechanical aspects of Kardecism—the prayers, paraphernalia, and invocations—as a re-placement for the egungun.

Although the philosophical aspects of Kardecism are virtually ignored in Santeria, the skill of becoming possessed by the spirits of the dead has become essential to every santero. Kardecian Spiritism does exist in Cuba, especially in the eastern city of Santiago, but it is as Santeria's new egungun that Kardecism has become part of the Afro-Cuban religious world. According to Lydia Cabrera,

> El espiritismo [cuenta] con miles y miles de creyentes y con miles y miles de mediums. Lo cual no supone debilitamiento de la fe en los orishas ni abandono de los cultos de raiz africana: el espiritismo marcha con ellos de la mano, estrechamente unidos . . .[5]

> ... Spiritism [has] thousands upon thousands of adherents and thousands upon thousands of mediums [in Cuba], yet this does not mean that faith in the orishas has weakened, nor have African-based cults been abandoned: Spiritism marches right along with them, hand in hand, closely allied . . .

Honoring the dead, often mistakenly labeled "ancestor worship," is of paramount importance in Santeria. As my old padrino used to say, "First come the dead, then Eleggua, then the other orishas." "But what about God?" I used to ask. "He is everywhere," was Padrino's answer. One of Lydia Cabrera's informants also reiterates the ascendancy of the ancestors over every other being:

> A los muertos hay que tenerlos contentos . . . el muerto en todas las reglas pare al santo . . . antes de saludar a los santos, se saluda a los muertos.[6]
>
> The dead need to be kept happy. . . . In all [Afro-Cuban] religions, the dead give birth to the orishas. . . . Before one pays respect to the orishas, one must honor the spirits of the dead.[6]

In modern Santeria, the dead are expected to be propitiated not only with the mandatory Catholic mass nine days after death, but with the *misa espiritual* (Spiritist mass), which is basically a Kardecian séance, as well. Kardec's *Selected Prayers* is also used as inspirational reading during times of grief and is found in every santero's home, although his more philosophical works are ignored in Santeria.

In Santeria, the focus of devotion to the ancestors is the *bóveda espiritual.* This is an altar made by covering a table with a white cloth and placing a number of clear glasses of water on top of it. Each glass of water represents a particular ancestor or spirit guide. A crucifix and photographs of the dear departed are also placed on top of the table. Spirit guides are often Lucumí or Congo spirits, Plains Indians, and gypsies. The appearance of Plains Indians in Cuban Santeria is curious, probably a direct contribution of nineteenth-century American spiritualism, where such Indian guides were common.

For a typical *misa*, a *bóveda* would be set up at the home of a medium as the focus of the gathering. Mediums and visitors, usually dressed in white, sit in chairs that have been placed so that all participants can see the glasses on top of the *bóveda*—many spiritists practice water gazing, a form of divination similar to gazing at a crystal ball. Holy water from a Catholic church, herbal water, and the cologne known as Florida water are made available. Those present take turns stepping up to the *bóveda* and putting one or all of these spiritual cleansers on their temples, hands, and other parts of their bodies; this action is believed to cleanse the participants of negative vibrations, preparing them to receive the spirits of the dead—preferably good spirits. After the opening prayers of Kardec's *Selected Prayers* are read, the spirits begin to possess the mediums. Elevated spirits give advice, while the backward spirits are helped through the prayers and incantations of the participants. Finally, closing prayers from Kardec's book are read and the *misa* comes to an end.

My first real encounter with Espiritismo occurred in 1963, about a year after my grandmother's death, when it was decided I should attend one of the *misas* being performed for the first anniversary of her death. Because I had been busy with my own duties as an iyabó (novitiate), I had not taken part in any of the earlier *misas*. The *misa* was to be performed at Amanda's house. As I entered the familiar house with my mother, I was surprised to feel a very different atmosphere, as if it were not the same place where I had received so much of my early teachings in Lucumí ways. The living room was arranged differently, with chairs placed in a circle and a table on the periphery of the circle serving as a central focus of the arrangement. The table was beautifully decorated with flowers, glasses of water, and candles. As soon as I spotted Amanda sitting next to the table I rushed to pay my respects in the Lucumí manner, but she seemed embarrassed; saying "God bless you" in Spanish, she told me to sit with my mother and aunt. I looked around the room and saw many familiar faces, such as Zena and Andres, but also numerous people I did not recognize, white people. I also noticed no one was wearing their emblematic necklaces.

As I sat between my aunt and my mother, I overheard them talking. "She shouldn't have been rude to the boy, how is he supposed to know that today she is not the great *iyalocha* but the consumate espiritista?" my aunt Haydée said.

"Shush, Haydée," my mother answered sharply "You shouldn't misjudge Madrina. You know many of these *blancos* would be turned off by Santeria—she has to cater to them."

After the preliminary prayers and ritual cleansings were performed, some very beautiful espiritista songs were sung in Spanish. Suddenly Zena convulsed and froze in a strange position with her eyes closed; all assembled focused on her. At the same time I felt a presence standing right behind me and a cold wind began to envelop me; my awareness of my surroundings became acutely sensitive. Zena opened her eyes and, looking straight at me, said, "There is a tremendously powerful spirit standing right behind Raulito. I think he is identifying himself as his guardian spirit."

My mother became very excited and fired questions at Zena: "Is it a good spirit? Is it a relative? Does it need light?"

Amanda motioned for my mother to be quiet. I felt the presence move closer to Zena. At least five of the sixteen people in attendance appeared to be following the same point, invisible to the others, with their eyes. I could not clearly see a form but knew exactly where it was.

Zena appeared terrified. "I've never seen anything like this except in movies. It's an old man of great beauty, his skin Amanda's color, but he is not African. He has a long, straight, full beard and long, straight white hair. His eyes are tranquil, he is wearing a long white robe, he looks a little like God the Father in Catholic churches."

My mother began to show fear. "If this spirit is so close to my son, I must know what he wants. At least tell me if he is a good spirit."

"I don't know, I can't tell, I've never seen anything like—Eeeeeegh!" Zena let out an agonizing screech, and Amanda sprinkled some holy water on her while reciting the Our Father. Zena removed the white scarf from her head and covered her face with it. She then sat up in a most natural fashion and began to speak in an unknown language. Everyone was totally baffled. Emma Rawlings, my mother's cook who was attending a *misa* for the first time, finally realized Zena was speaking English in a strange accent and could understand what the being that had possessed Zena was saying. Emma, who was Jamaican-born, said that she had met Trinidadians of East Indian descent in Jamaica who spoke with an accent similar to that used by the entity.

A visitor said, "How can Zena be speaking English? I know her for years, she can barely speak Spanish!" After a few chuckles,

Amanda said that although the phenomenon we were witnessing was rarely seen (most spirits could speak in the language of their hosts), sometimes they chose to speak in a language unknown to the medium in order to prove the reality of their presence and to dispel fears of fraud or self-deception.

I was fascinated by how Zena had changed. Her posture was regal and yet so natural. In the white scarf that covered her face I clearly saw the face of the bearded, long-haired man she had described, as if a moving picture was being projected on the white cloth. Emma became an important actor in the strange play that began to unravel, for she served as interpreter. The being made this statement (my mother still has notes from that day):

> Greetings. May peace and understanding be with each and every one of you. This is the only time I will allow my presence to intrude in a gathering such as this one, but I must say a few words of warning. I am Maha Bagwan Manusthava, and I am karmically linked to that young man [he pointed to me]. This killing of animals and pursuit of magic through blood is not for him; it is not his path. Keep him away from all meats, feed him the fruits the earth willingly gives. Someday he will know why I came this day.

The spirit then looked straight at me, and all of a sudden I felt as if the entire room was blacked out and only he and I were there, were real. He told me, "Whenever you feel desperate or sad or need comfort, repeat over and over, 'Peace, be still, and know that I am God.' Do this, and you'll never be defeated." To this day, repeating the phrase that the spirit gave me so long ago calms me and puts me in a meditative state as no other words can.

After the spirit had departed, leaving behind a totally baffled group of Cuban spiritists and santeros, Zena reported a feeling of total bliss: "I haven't felt so good in years."

My mother was agitated. "That Manitoba guy, whatever his name, must be an evil spirit—otherwise he would not have spoken against our religion, which is what he did." Amanda tried to bring the séance back to order, but everyone was too confused to concentrate. She then abruptly began to read the closing prayers and ended the *misa*. After all outsiders had departed, my aunt asked Amanda, "Madrina, what the hell was that all about? Was it an *espiritu burlón* [poltergeist]?"

Amanda lit one of her small cigars, and puffing slowly, said, "In the fifty-some years I have been a spiritist, I have seen dark spirits bad-mouthing religion, good spirits recommending someone to follow a religious path, but never a good spirit bad-mouthing our religion. How did he get through our spirit guardians, most of which were santeros in life? And what kind of life was he recommending for the boy, not eating meat? I never heard of such a thing."

"What should we do, Madrina? Is that spirit going to be bad for the boy?"

Zena interjected, "I don't know what happened, 'cause I was out while that old man took my body, but I can assure you that he is not a bad spirit. In fact, in my seventy-two years as a medium, I have never hosted a higher being."

"Not even the orishas?" my mother asked. "I was talking as a spiritist; *ocha* (the Siete Potencias) is altogether a different thing."

After taking long puffs on her cigar, softly chanting to Obatalá to grant her wisdom, Amanda finally said, "I'm confused; we had better consult Ifá on this." It was agreed that my mother and our party would spend the night at Amanda's; the next day we would all drive to Luyanó to consult the oracle of Ifá with Padrino.

I was so taken with what "Manitoba" had said that I refused to eat the ham sandwich Amanda prepared for breakfast. I wanted to do as he had instructed, which upset my mother. "You must eat meat or you'll die!"

In Luyanó, after Padrino consulted the table of Ifá, he said, "That was not a bad spirit, and he will always be around the boy no matter what we do. He was like an uninvited guest who doesn't understand what he has walked into. If he is to be a guide for our boy this must not happen now, for the boy would not be able to understand the teachings of such a spirit and would probably lose his reason. I feel, however, that it is Raul's destiny to meet with Manitoba again. For now, however, I will make sure Manitoba doesn't appear in the near future." I was not to hear from Manitoba again until my thirteenth birthday—but that is a different story.

Amanda felt bad about the way things had gone at the *misa*, so she volunteered to set up a second séance "free of charge" to give the spirit of my grandmother a chance to speak. What I witnessed at that séance—and have corroborated with the accounts of many of those who were there—can only be described as paranormal or supernatural.

A spirit said to be my grandmother possessed Amanda. The relatives gathered at the *misa* were unimpressed and in fact doubted the sincerity of the spiritist, for Grandmama did not speak as she normally would have and did not call any of us by the pet names she used. She just said that she missed us and was still not content with being dead. After the uneventful visit of my purported Grandmama, however, a spirit claiming to be her father took over Ines, a tiny, rather portly woman. This visitation really astounded my relatives, for Ines spoke as my great-grandfather spoke and knew things she couldn't possibly know. "I was a big man, bigger than you," the spirit said, looking at a relative who weighed 260 pounds and stood six feet, three inches tall. "In fact, I'll prove it to you." With that, the tiny woman—Ines could not have been more than four feet, ten inches tall—picked the huge man up in a seemingly effortless manner and carried him on her back, running around the room and laughing.

The next spirit to make his appearance was Zena's guide, a long-dead Congo who loved to drink *aguardiente*. Since Zena was famous for her spirit guide, who drank enormous amounts of aguardiente while in his hostess' body, a relative of mine who thought the whole thing a fraud had brought a gallon of Bacardi rum to the séance. When little Zena, then almost eighty, became possessed by Francisco Tatabu, she gave the impression of being tall and strong. Her normally soft, sweet voice became hoarse and masculine. When the spirit demanded aguardiente, my relative told him he had brought some Bacardi rum for him. "White man's *malafo* is weak like water, but I'll drink it."

Zena—or the spirit who possessed her—then gulped down the entire gallon of Bacardi without stopping. She then said, "That wasn't bad, but now I want to go outside." She ran out with amazing speed, and the entire gathering followed her. To silence those who would doubt her, Zena then announced that she was going to fly. With an agility impossible for an old woman, Zena climbed up a side of the house and stood on the roof—which admittedly was not that high, about seven feet. She said, "Here I come," dived to the ground as if she were diving into a pool, and appeared to land on her side. I flinched and many people covered their eyes with their hands, but Zena then got up and began to sing and dance a mambo—the Congo kind, not the popular dance derived from it—a very funny mambo that went, "Pluma de cotora colorá, que boníta, pluma de cotora colorá" (red parrot feather, how pretty, red parrot feather). Soon everyone was singing and a strange feeling of joy overtook everyone present. After the *misa* was over, Zena was her own little sweet self again and did not show any inebriation in her speech or actions.

Years later, trying to reconstruct what had happened, I heard some really ludicrous accounts of how Zena had flown around the hut that day. The nonbelievers who were present, however, concurred with me that the woman did drink a gallon of 80-proof rum, that she later leaped from the roof of Amanda's house to the ground, and that after her trance, no sign of her drinking was noticeable. Such inexplicable events are common in the world of Santeria, as they are in any system that does not shut out the supernatural.

NOTES

1. See Candido Procopio Ferreira de Camargo, *Kardecismo e Umbanda: Una interpretaçao sociologica* [Kardecism and Umbanda: A Sociological Interpretation] (Sao Paolo, 1961).

2. For the particulars of Kardec's life, I relied on Lisias Nogueira Negrao's "Kardecism," *Encyclopedia of Religion*, vol. 8 (New York: Macmillan, 1987), 259-261.

3. Ibid.

4. Lydia Cabrera, *La Sociedad secreta abakuá* [The Abakuá Secret Society] (Miami: Coleccion del Chichereku, 1970), 33.

5. Cabrera, *El Monte* [The Bush] (Miami: Coleccion del Chichereku, 1986), 29-30.

6. Ibid., 62.

O Mío, Yemayá!
Mixed media (watercolor, acrylic), 16" x 22"

Priestess possessed by Yemayá. "How fortunate are the Santeros! While others pray to an invisible god hoping someday to see him, the Divine is manifested in Santeria as living, breathing beings."

Shangó
Mixed media (acrylic, tempera, ink, photography), 108" x 54"

Shangó is the lord of thunder and lightning, lord of drumming and dancing, and the epitome of manly beauty.

Oshún
Mixed media (watercolor, ink)
8" x 10"
From the collection of
Professor Cheryl Townsend-Gilkes,
Colby College, Maine

Oshún
Acrylic, 50" x 54"

Oshún, queen of rivers, epitomizes female beauty and sensuality.

El Despojo
Acrylic, 24" x 36"

Plants are used in Santeria in what are called *despojos*. In a despojo, a person or place is spiritually cleansed by having the right herbs or plants passed over his or her body.

Eleggua
Mixed media, 12" x 18"

Lord of the crossroads, Eleggua is the divine messenger of God Almighty
and the orisha who opens up the doors of progress.

Photographs by Raul Canizares

Top: One of the many *botánicas* found in West Tampa.

Bottom left: Imagery from the Plains Indians in Cuban Santeria is curious; it is probably a direct contribution of nineteenth-century American spiritualism.

Bottom right: When this image of Saint Barbara/Shangó was paraded, followers of Santeria could worship Shangó publicly without being detected by the Catholic authorities.

Women Dancing
Hand-painted photograph, 8" x 10"

"The long tables where everyone had feasted were removed, and the whole backyard became a temple where everyone danced for the orishas."

Ogún
Mixed media, 18" x 24"

Ogún, the divine blacksmith, gave humankind the power to forge iron. He is also the eternal rival of Shangó.

CHAPTER 9

EBBÓ:
SACRIFICE

On a television program I once saw a well-meaning medical examiner from a city in southern Florida, where many followers of Santeria live, earnestly imploring believers to stop the barbaric practice of animal sacrifice. He went on to say that if "Santerians [*sic*]" gave up the practice of animal sacrifice, they would be "welcomed to the family of civilized religions."[1] In New York City, a santero named El Akoni, who has a considerable number of followers, has publicly renounced the practice of animal sacrifice. In Miami, famous santero Carlos Canet has also given up blood sacrifices. As admirable as these santeros' decisions to practice Santeria without blood may appear, the consensus among other santeros is that, whatever it is they are doing, they are not doing Santeria. For most santeros, a practitioner who gives up animal sacrifice is an apostate.

Without a doubt, in the United States the practice of animal sacrifice has caused the greatest number of misunderstandings between believers in Santeria and nonbelievers. Santeros think a society that condones the mass slaughter of animals, often under apalling conditions, to simply eat their flesh has no right to criticize the ritual slaughter of animals for religious reasons. Our present-day Western culture consistently practices what may be the most cruel and inhumane treatment of animals of any culture in recorded history. The subjugation and exploitation of animals for research and the conditions on mass-breeding farms create a level of cruelty that is unimaginable and unconscionable in the eyes of indigenous cultures that over the ages have maintained a balance and sense of purpose in their hunting and animal sacrifice practices. In these cultures, the empathetic relationship between humans and animals—characterized by affection and respect, telepathic communication, deification of animals as messengers of the divine, and actual killings for sacrifice and for food—defines their actions and their place in the universe. These attitudes are typical of Yoruba culture, the womb from which Santeria emerged.

To take an intellectual, judgmental view of animal sacrifice is hypocritical; in our society all of us, even vegetarian animal-rights activists, must admit to being supported by an infrastructure that thrives on the inhumane treatment of animals. All of nature is built on a cycle of life and death that affects every life form, from the simplest to the most complex. Every breath we take sacrifices tens of thousands of microscopic organisms. But instead of seeing death as inherent in the life experience, our society looks at death as a problem to be overcome by some human invention or to be removed from everyday experience. This attitude obfuscates our relationship with death, reducing it to a very pedestrian level.

In *El Santo (La Ocha)*, Julio García Cortez tells the story of how, after humankind lost communion with God, humans were dispersed throughout the world. At that time God (Olodumare) first allowed people to use animals for food after first spilling their blood on the earth as a sign of thanksgiving.[2] Joseph Murphy, on the other hand, sees sacrifice as the Santeria practitioner's way of deepening the relationship with the orishas: "In gifts of animals and plants, human beings honor the orishas and dispose them to offer gifts in return. Life for life, ashé for ashé, humans grow in the divine exchange of energy."[3] Blood is thought in Santeria to carry enormous amounts of ashé, or spiritual power. The fundamental stones that in Santeria are thought to be repositories of the orishas' ashé, as well as many other implements, need periodic sprinklings of sacrificial blood in order to remain efficacious, or "alive."

Animal sacrifice in Santeria is not practiced as often as some people suppose. Large mammals are extremely rarely sacrificed, since relatively few priests—only specially trained babalaos—possess the right to kill such animals. Sacrifice in Santeria is performed for several reasons and can vary from the very simple (a bunch of red bananas for Shangó) to the very complex (several goats, hens, and chickens used in an initiation). Although all sacrifices are technically termed ebbós, some santeros call the simpler ones addimus.

There are five basic types of sacrifice in Santeria: thanksgiving, propitiatory, preventive, initiatory, and substitution.[4] In some cases a sacrifice may have elements of two or more of these types. Generally speaking, humans only partake of the flesh of animals that have been slain in thanksgiving or initiatory ceremonies. Carcasses from other sacrifices are disposed of in a variety of ways, not all of them acceptable to modern American society.

Thanksgiving offerings range from a simple fruit placed in front of an image of an orisha to large feasts where hundreds of animals are killed and cooked for hundreds of guests. They are made either in gratitude for general good fortune or for specific favors obtained from the orishas. Propitiatory sacrifices are deemed necessary when an orisha demands to be appeased. This may be because the *omo* (devotee) has neglected his or her duties to an orisha or for some less tangible reason. Animals sacrificed for propitiatory purposes are almost never eaten. Preventive sacrifices are similar to propitionary ones, except that they are performed *before* the orishas ask for them.

Initiatory sacrifices are performed during the course of an initiation ceremony. The sometimes huge quantities of animals slain at kariocha initiations are always eaten by guests at the three-day feast where a new santero or santera is presented to the world. Animals sacrificed at lesser initiations, such as the fowl killed at the collares initiation ceremony, are generally not consumed by humans.

Substitution sacrifices offer an animal in place of a human life that is in danger. I remember going with my mother to see our old padrino for a routine reading when I was six years old. Padrino's ebony skin turned pale when he saw in his *tablero* (divining board) what lay ahead of me. "Death is claiming the child," Padrino told my mother. "The *letra* (sign) is so strong I don't know if I can break it." Padrino began to ask Ifá what ebbó was required, starting with the simplest. He was pleased to find out that only a black rooster for Ogún was needed. He immediately went to his backyard and picked out the unfortunate bird that would lose his life for me. After he poured the consecrated blood of the sacrificed animal on me, Padrino's oracle informed him that the sacrifice had been accepted and my life would be spared. "Go home and do not let him out of your sight," Padrino told my mother. "Something bad may still happen to him, but his life will be spared."

When we reached our bus stop after the ride home, the bus driver opened the door before coming to a complete halt. I was riding on my mother's lap; when I jumped up and ran out, I slipped and my leg went under the huge bus' front tires. Fortunately a pothole provided some room for my tiny foot, for I only suffered a tire burn. I still have the scar to remind me of that freak accident. The sacrifice called for by Ifá was uncanny, since in some parts of Africa, people who die in vehicular accidents are said to have been taken away by Ogún.

Many santeros feel that before Santeria can be accepted as a "real" religion, the animal sacrifice issue must be resolved. Concerned civil authorities in certain areas of southern Florida have tried to work out an agreement with a group of santeros so that they can maintain their religious practices without violating the legal and moral codes accepted by American society in general. Basically, the santeros have been offered the freedom to practice animal sacrifice as long as (1) the government can make sure no animals suffer; (2) the meat of sacrificed animals is used for food; (3) only animals normally used for food are slaughtered; and (4) carcasses are disposed of properly. This may sound fair, but I contend that santeros will find these terms impossible to accept. From a santero's perspective, the first condition is easily met; Santeria priests who perform sacrifices could be licensed and subject to state supervision to make sure animals are humanely slaughtered. The second condition is impossible. Although some prominent santeros have defended the practice of animal sacrifice by saying that after the blood of such animals has been offered to the orishas, the flesh is consumed by the santeros, this is only true of certain types of sacrifice. In reality, the great majority of carcasses of animals sacrificed in Santeria do not end up on the dinner table. Ninety percent of animals slain in Santeria sacrifices fall into the category required by the third condition, but sometimes this or that orisha will demand an animal that is not usually used for human consumption. The fourth condition will also be difficult to satisfy, since a santero will usually not know where a carcass is to be deposited until the orisha is consulted after the sacrifice is performed. Possible sites could be by a railway, at a crossroads, by a cemetery, in a cornfield, or by a large tree. Obviously, most of these places would be deemed inappropriate by mainstream American standards, yet unless the carcass is disposed of in the manner prescribed by the orisha, the whole sacrifice is considered useless.

Frankly, I do not foresee an easy solution to the sacrifice problem. Proper disposal of the carcasses may yet prove to be the most difficult issue to resolve; santeros will probably continue to be persecuted over this for years to come. What may happen is that an offshoot of Santeria that gives up animal sacrifice will become more popular, though whether a tradition so devoted to the practice of animal sacrifice can survive such a change is something only time will tell. Another possibility is that santeros will find ingenious loopholes, such as designating certain crossroads for disposal of the carcasses that could be monitored by city personnel. Santeros will need to engage in this type of speculation to eventually find an acceptable solution, but the outlook is not hopeless. As Africans once proved in Cuba and as Cubans have proved in southern Florida, the followers of Santeria are a resourceful people, well able to adapt to conditions around them.

NOTES

1. The physician in question has asked me not to publish his name; he has since changed his position and says he would be embarrassed by how "foolishly naive"—his words—he was.

2. Julio García Cortez, *El Santo (La Ocha)* [The Saints: Ocha], 3d ed. (Miami: Ediciones Universal, 1983), 97–105.

3. Joseph M. Murphy, *Santeria: An African Religion in America* (Boston: Beacon Press, 1988), 15.

4. I have adapted these categories from J. Osmorade Awolalu, *Yoruba Beliefs and Sacrificial Rites* (London: Longman, 1979), 143.

CHAPTER 10

THE SECRET OF THE WEREWOLF

After my kariocha initiation, I had daily lessons with my padrino during my iyabó (novitiate) year. Sometimes he would tell me of great secrets that had been lost, of the powers that allowed men and women to become beasts. During this period I had often dreamed that I was an owl; I asked Padrino whether I would be an owl if I could learn how to become a beast. He looked at me and slowly nodded his head up and down. "You are an owl, just as I am a turkey buzzard (*aura tiñosa*)," he said.

The belief that some people have the capacity to transform into other animal species exists in many cultures; in fact, in *The Origin of the Werewolf Superstition* Caroline Taylor Stewart states that "the belief that a human being is capable of assuming an animal's form is an almost worldwide superstition."[1] She continues, "The werewolf superstition is an old one, a primitive one. The point in common everywhere is the transformation of a living human being into an animal, into a wolf in regions where the wolf was common; into a lion, hyena or leopard in Africa."[2] Although such beliefs are not central in Afro-Cuban culture, they are recurrent and widespread enough to merit some investigation.

Afro-Cuban lore is replete with tales of powerful santeros and Ñáñigos who possessed the power to turn into animals at will. This was felt to be especially true of the Ñáñigos, who are descendants of the legendary Leopard People. Originally from the Calabar region of West Africa, the Leopard People were members of Efik-speaking tribes. They were said to have the power to turn into animals, particularly wolves or leopards. In Cuba some of these stories were told of the Ñáñigos, although it was widely believed that the power to transform oneself into a nonhuman species was lost. In Haiti, tales of the *loupgarou,* the man-wolf, abound.

Cuban authorities erroneously believed that to accomplish the metamorphosis, the Ñáñigos required the fat of white babies. This preposterous notion probably reflected European views on witchcraft and had nothing to do with any of the African cultures that survived in Cuba.

One very old Santeria practitioner reputed to have the power to turn into an animal was my own padrino, Juan García. He had the power to turn into a turkey buzzard; he had acquired this knowledge not from his tradition but from a Native American from Mexico.

"It was right after a singer you know of became famous—with my help of course," Padrino said. "Mexico was the first country outside Cuba that recognized his enormous talent, so after he signed to make records with RCA-Mexico, he asked me to go with him on an extended tour of that wonderful land." Puffing on his cigar, his large, dark eyes misty, Padrino seemed lost in some long-forgotten memory. He continued, "It was 1948; I was not so old that the glamour of show business would be lost on me." He chuckled. "My friend toured all through Mexico with tremendous success. In a small town in the state of Oaxaca, however, my attention was diverted from show business to religion. I had taken a bus tour of some of the Indian villages of the area. While I was walking with the rest of the group, a young boy tugged at my jacket sleeve and asked me if I was Juan García. I told him I was, and he asked me to follow him. He led me to a small wooden hut. Inside, there was some kind of an altar made up of several wooden steps leading almost to the roof. It was covered in sequined red, white, and green clothes, on top of which were placed dozens of lighted candles. It dominated the entire room. At the bottom of this strange altar were numerous herbs I recognized as well as some I did not. I instinctively touched the floor with my fingertips, kissing them afterward, as a sign of respect. An Indian man slightly older than me, dressed in a somewhat worn brown suit and a bowler hat and puffing on a Havana cigar, extended his hand to me.

'Welcome to my house, Don Juan. I am Torino, and I think we may learn some things from each other.'

'I'm sorry, sir,' I said, startled, 'but how do you know my name?'

Laughing heartily, Torino said that he was padrino of a Mexican singer, who was touring with my singer friend, and that she had told him all about me and my great powers."

Padrino continued, "'I ought to be jealous,' Torino told me. 'Sandra tells me that your friend gave her a charm based on your recipes, that has greatly helped her career.'

I replied, 'I have a number of show business people among my godchildren and clients. I guess I've developed some charms that have some efficacy in that area.' Torino asked me, 'Come, Juan, sit with me and share my food; we must talk padrino to padrino.' He went on, 'Cuban Santeria is thought to be extremely powerful for obtaining monetary rewards. Is this so?'

I responded, 'I've heard that Mexican *curanderos* can cure any disease and that some have the power to turn into animals. Is that so?'

Torino then surprised me by saying a phrase I guess I didn't expect an Indian *curandero* to know: 'I see you want a quid pro quo, my friend. All right, for these show-business charms, which disease should I teach you how to cure?'

"'I do fine curing people, Don Torino. It is this business of turning into a beast that interests me.'

"Don Torino replied, 'If anyone else had asked me to show them that particular *secreto,* I would have laughed, but you are a man of wisdom—more developed than me in some areas, judging by the brightness of your aura. I think I can teach you the *secreto* in three days.'

I said, 'That is exactly the time required for me to teach you how to make the amulets you wish to learn how to make.' With that, we both shook hands, and in three days we each had what we wanted."

After a long pause, when it was obvious to me Padrino was not going on, I begged him to tell me more. He refused. "I don't care how proud your parents are of your genius I.Q., little one, there are some things a seven-year-old can't grasp, no matter how bright he is. Besides, you are not all that smart, you are just lucky enough to have Obatalá constantly whispering in your ear."

I felt somewhat dejected and almost started to cry, for I was all ready to learn how to become an owl. Noticing my disappointment, Padrino stroked my hair and said, smiling, "I won't teach you how to become an owl just yet, but I'll do the next best thing. Today after dinner, go to your special grove, the one where you learned to walk with the Night, and take a *siesta.*"

That afternoon I did as I was told and I had a most vivid dream of being a large owl, flying up and down the island of Cuba, visiting towns and villages I had never seen before. I woke up elated and satisfied that, at least for a while, I had become an owl.

Four years were to pass before Padrino brought up the subject again. "I've known since your itá that you are not to remain in Cuba, that I will pass from the material plane while you are beyond the waters. For this reason, I've deposited most of my secrets with Rey, who is older and better able to guard them. Someday, however, Rey, your older brother in religion, will pass them on to you." Rey, who became a babalao the same week I made saint, was about ten years older than me. He was a serious student of Ifá who came from a long line of babalaos. Years later I would serve a period of apprenticeship with him in New Orleans, where as Ifá P. he became a powerful religious leader. When the moment seemed right, I asked Padrino again if he could really turn into a turkey buzzard. "'Reality' is a word of little meaning," Padrino said. "I could tell you of hundreds of people who have died when, while in the guise of an animal, they have been killed by others who did not know they were killing a human."

"Padrino," I asked, "years ago you told me that a Mexican *curandero* named Torino taught you how to become a buzzard. Can you tell me if this is so?"

Becoming somewhat annoyed, Padrino told me, "Let's put it this way. If a buzzard ever comes around you, don't harm it because it could possibly be me trying to help you, and were you to cause any harm to that buzzard, the same harm would be suffered by me."

For years after my emigration to the United States in 1966, I often thought of what I jokingly called the "werewolf question." In 1972, while fishing in Lake Pontchartrain in New Orleans with Ifá P., I finally got an answer. He told me, "What the Mexican taught our old Padrino was a technique of identification with a particular animal. It was a question of extreme focus."

"Are all Mexican *curanderos* able to turn into animals?" I asked my friend.

"According to Padrino, Don Torino was no *curandero*, he was a—uhm—I can't say the word. I promised Padrino I would never repeat it." (Years later I found out the word Ifá P. would not utter was "devil-man".) "Anyway, he was something else. Don Torino showed our padrino how to achieve a particular kind of altered state by drinking an infusion made by boiling certain mushrooms and roots while chanting certain Indian incantations. Through this technique, a person's will can virtually enter into an animal, so that such a person can actually see through that animal's eyes and walk, fly, or swim inside the animal; it is as if, by some psychic mechanism, the animal acts as a television camera; whatever it sees is transmitted to you. In other words, it's a case of total identification with a particular animal. If something happens to that animal, the person in the trance will suffer a shock and possibly die."

So that was it! A kind of altered state, a supersensitive type of telepathy. Suddenly, the idea of a man turning into an animal did not seem so farfetched. Can't a person send his voice over thousands of miles with the use of a telephone? As one who had experienced thousands of what skeptics would call "so-called supernatural events," I considered this new revelation most appropriate.

More recently, I met a follower of the Mexican "devil-man" Torino who knew of his generosity toward my padrino. She shed some light on why Torino would divulge to Padrino such a great secret. "Torino *was* a devil-man (*diablero*)," my informant said. "A devil-man is not necessarily evil, just someone who can turn into a beast. Torino was—and still is—also an avid reader who loves to learn about the impact Europeans made on peoples of color. For years Torino read about the demise of his own people, the Indians, from the Caribbean and about how the African races were able to retain their culture in Cuba and Brazil. He also read about the Leopard People of Calabar and their descendants in Cuba, who forgot how to turn into leopards. By teaching Juan his techniques, Torino felt he was giving back to the Leopard People something they had lost."

The story of Torino's gift to my padrino is significant on several levels. It exemplifies the willingness of a representative of one indigenous people to share what he perhaps considered his greatest treasure with a representative of an indigenous culture different from his own. It also exemplifies how some basic beliefs appear to be held in common by widely diverse groups. The so-called werewolf question, for example, has been found to form a part of the lore of the Lapps, Finns, North Asiatic peoples, Native Americans, and Africans, as well as Indians and people from Borneo. It exists in highly industrialized societies where people often forget how tied down to earth we all really are and, for that matter, how tied down we are to one another's destinies. As Padrino used to say, "Don't kill a fly if you don't have to, for you never know what potentate sits behind it." The rather obscure proverb—it does lose something in the translation—refers to the food chain and how we should be careful not to cause a species' extinction, since we may never know if that species, no matter how apparently insignificant, may form the basis of a huge pyramid at the top of which we teeter.

NOTES

1. Caroline Taylor Stewart, *The Origin of the Werewolf Superstition* (Columbia: University of Missouri Press, 1909), i.

2. Ibid., 4-5.

CHAPTER 11

EWE ORISHA:
THE USE OF HERBS AND PLANTS IN SANTERIA

The information contained in this chapter is the result of years of learning at the feet of many masters. I can no longer recall with certainty who said what when. Three people, however, merit special mention because of their selfless sharing of precious knowledge. They are the late babalaos Juan García and Paco Cuevas and the unforgettable Amanda Gomez of Mantilla.

Maferefún e ibae (thanks and peace to them).

All santeros are herbalists, and some possess a truly amazing knowledge of the medicinal qualities of plants. Anyone even marginally acquainted with Santeria has heard of or knows about a seemingly miraculous cure effected by a santero after conventional medical science had given up. Santeria, however, does not reject science; a santera or santero will sometimes recommend seeing a doctor for an operation or other conventional treatment, first preparing the patient with *omiero,* a magical herbal infusion. Sometimes, however, a Santeria cure can make major interventions like surgery unnecessary. For example, while hosting a radio talk show in 1984 I suddenly lost my voice; talking became excruciatingly painful. A throat specialist told me I needed an emergency operation, but my mother made an infusion of some common weeds she called *romerillo.* After gargling with the infusion for a few days, my voice was back to normal.

In the case of Elena, which took place in the 1950s, Santeria was used to counteract the effects of an evil spell that had stymied her physicians. Elena had been married for fifteen years when she began to notice a change in her husband. He often came home late and his clothes reeked of a strange perfume. Although Elena tried to ignore the situation, hoping it would resolve itself, gossip reached her that her husband was having an affair with a Haitian woman said to be a practitioner of Vodun, which many Cubans unfairly equate with evil sorcery. Although she was black, Elena was a devout Catholic who did not participate in any of the Afro-Cuban religions. One day, after eating a grapefruit her husband had brought her, Elena became violently ill and had to be rushed to the hospital. In the emergency room, Elena's abdomen swelled to incredible proportions. Some of the best physicians in Havana were confounded by Elena's case. The doctors had trouble diagnosing, much less treating, Elena's condition. After she had languished near death in a hospital room for several days, her abdomen swollen to the point of bursting, Elena's family was called in for a conference.

The oldest of the three physicians present said that they had done all that they could and that Elena would only live a few more hours. After the older doctor and a younger assistant had left the room, the remaining physician, a young black man, spoke to the relatives. "I could get in trouble for telling you this, but I don't think she has a 'regular' disease, if you know what I mean. If I were you I'd seek help of a different kind." The young doctor's veiled words were immediately understood by a relative who believed in Santeria. Elena's resolve not to resort to Santeria crumbled in the face of imminent death, and her family called in Concha, a legendary santera and healer.

The raggedy white woman looked out of place among the well-dressed friends and relatives who were keeping a death vigil over Elena. Her face showed the ravages of leprosy, which caused some to look away in disgust. Approaching Elena, who was by then turning purple, Concha said, "These doctors can't help you, girl. You are the victim of a *burundanga*, an evil spell. Your husband took some fruit intended for you to his mistress' house. She's an evil *bruja* (sorceress); without him knowing, she injected the fruit with *polvo de sapo*, a poison made out of dried toad. That's why you're bursting like a toad." Searching in a dirty sackcloth bag, Concha took out a dark green bottle filled with liquid. "Drink two gulps of this each morning before you drink anything else. This is omiero, the holy liquid of the orishas—it's made out of herbs and other stuff you don't want to know about. Just make sure you drink it like I told you and by the time you finish the bottle, you'll be fine." The female relative who brought in the santera tried to push a fifty-peso note into her hand but Concha refused, saying, "I can only charge $1.05 for my services, but when Elena gets better, have her bring some flowers and candles to my altar for my santos."

Almost immediately Elena's health began to improve. She finished up the foul-smelling, cloudy substance in seven days, following Concha's instructions. The next night, over twelve gallons of a foul-smelling liquid—"exactly like the omiero" Elena had been drinking, according to an eyewitness—was drained out of Elena's abdomen. Two days later, Elena walked out of the hospital to the amazement of her physicians. Elena became a believer in Santeria and went to Concha seeking initiation. To Elena's surprise, Concha refused to initiate her into the religion. "The orishas do not claim you; you may offer them flowers and food, but you are not meant to be a santera." Elena continued to seek Concha's counsel for many years afterward.

PLANTS AND THE ORISHAS

Lydia Cabrera named her monumental work on plants in Santeria *El Monte* [The Bush] because the wilderness is the true repository of all of Santeria's secrets.[1] Plants, especially herbs, are essential to every Santeria ritual; as a matter of fact they play a much greater role in the religion than animal sacrifice. Each plant is said to be owned by a specific orisha (or orishas). When a plant is used for medicinal or ritualistic purposes, a santero must know what orisha needs to be petitioned for it. Although each orisha has ownership of particular plants, two orishas, Inle and Osain, have lordship over all plants.

Older santeros tell me that originally Inle owned all plants but that he later ceded this power to Osain, who had a more encompassing knowledge of the magical properties of plants, as opposed to Inle's knowledge of the curative powers of herbs.[2] Inle is thought to be an enormously powerful orisha, one who rarely possesses his devotees. Lydia Cabrera mentions a society of lesbians in nineteenth-century Cuba dedicated to the worship of Inle.[3] Inle demands sexual abstinence from his priests and priestesses (who must be women who are not of menstruating age). Apparently, the group Cabrera mentions did not feel their sexual practices fell under those forbidden by Inle. In modern Santeria, Inle is not commonly mentioned. For all intents and purposes, Osain is the one lord of all plants, the king of the bush.

Osain has no mother and no father; he sprang up from the soil. He usually keeps to himself, although he is very fond of Shangó. Osain is very conscious of the way he looks. He is malformed, having only one foot, one eye, and one arm. His ears are asymmetrical, one very big and deaf, the other tiny but so hypersensitive it can hear a leaf fall on the other side of the world. His oversized head is usually hidden behind a mask of straw. Like Ochosi, Osain is a master hunter. He can shoot an arrow better than any two-armed bowman.

How Osain came to look the way he does is a matter of debate. Paco Cuevas told me Osain was born that way so that he could always remember his other half is the bush. Juan García said Osain lost his limbs in a fight with Orula, who later had to beg him for forgiveness when Orula needed herbs. Osain loves Eleggua, and the trickster god is very fond of his deformed friend, never making him the brunt of his well-known pranks. Santeros believe some people are "born with the gift of Osain." These *osainistas* can work with herbs without having to undergo any kind of initiation.

Traditionally, many ilés in Havana held that the proper way for a santero or santera to obtain herbs was from a babalao, who in turn got them from an *osainista*. However, few ilés still follow this procedure. In the United States, santeros usually buy their plants at the local *botánica*. As well as the medicinal qualities santeros believe plants possess, many plants also are imbued with powerful magical qualities that can only be unleashed by certain practitioners such as priests and sorcerers. They are used both for ritual purposes and to cast spells.

"I sing to Osain when I work with herbs," Amanda used to say. "I won't wash *collares* unless I sing seven *suyeres* (prayers) to Osain." Washing collares is the act of infusing Santeria's emblematic necklaces with power (ashé) by ritually washing them in omiero water, the herbal infusion par excellence. Omiero usually has twenty-one herbs in it, though the amount of herbs can change depending on which orisha is involved. It is not easy to manufacture omiero. "Omiero must never be made with tap water," Amanda used to say. "I use rainwater collected from a crevice in the sacred iroko (silk cotton) tree during the month of May, river water collected on the feast of Saint John (June 24), and seawater collected on the early morning of Holy Saturday."

Omiero, a soothing, refreshing liquid, is supposed to be free of violent vibrations, and traditionally it was thought that women made the best omiero, since they were considered to be more peaceable than war-loving men. Washing collares is still an activity reserved for fully initiated santeras. Other herbal infusions and baths, however, can be prepared and used by any believer.

Aside from the uses we have so far discussed, plants are also used in Santeria in what are called *despojos*. In a despojo, a person or place is spiritually cleansed by having the right herbs or plants passed over his or her body or, in the case of a place, by striking the walls of the place with a bunch of the right plants. Despojos are said to work on two levels: by frightening away evil spirits and by conferring on the person positive energy. When a santera or santero carries out a despojo, she or he usually learns from an oracle or through inspiration which herbs are to be used and then strikes the person to be cleansed with a bunch of the herbs or plants as if it were a lash. The plants are said to attract all negative vibrations, leaving only the positive ones. Herbal baths, on the other hand, are prescribed by santeros for specific situations, such as improving luck, attracting a mate, or finding a job. The following are some commonly prescribed baths.

To improve one's luck, gather some basil (preferably fresh), lily flowers, and white roses in a pail of water and let them soak a few minutes. Although no number is specified, five or seven of each are generally considered adequate. After showering, pour this mixture over your body. Repeat for three days. Another recipe for good luck calls for adding leaves from an almond tree to bath water. Still another good-luck bath consists of adding lilies, white or yellow bell-like flowers called elecampane, rose water, and orange blossoms to the bath water—quantities are not specified—and bathing in it. It should be repeated eight consecutive days.

Oshún's own aphrodisiac bath consists of adding five yellow roses, five cinnamon sticks, and five teaspoons of honey to the bath water. Oshún's prescription to attract money is to bathe in water that contains five yellow roses, a bunch of parsley, some basil, five drops of five different perfumes, and five teaspoons of honey.

These are but a few of the many uses santeros give to herbs and plants. Lydia Cabrera's *El Monte* contains hundreds of herbal recipes. There is still much medical knowledge trapped in these and other ancient formulas. Luckily, the field of ethnobotany is growing; many of Santeria's ancient recipes, like rinsing the hair with chamomile, have been proved scientifically valid. This is certainly an area that deserves serious attention.

Table 1 lists some of the herbs and plants used in Santeria, the English name (when known), the orisha who owns the plant, and the condition(s) each plant supposedly alleviates. Santeros generally do not emphasize exact quantities except when specified by tradition. For most teas, a rule of thumb is one teaspoon of dried leaves or an equivalent amount of the fresh plant per cup of water.

TABLE 1. HERBS AND THEIR USES IN SANTERIA

Spanish name	English name	Ruling orisha	Medicinal or other uses
Almendro	Almond tree	Obatalá	Almond oil clears skin blemishes. Tea made by boiling the bark eliminates worms and parasites from the body.
Anis	Anise seed	Oshún	Anise seed tea calms an upset stomach and nervousness, eliminates fatigue.
Acacia	Acacia	Obatalá	Tea made of the roots and leaves eliminates fatigue.
Albahaca	Basil	All orishas	Crushed in a mortar and directly applied, it reduces swelling. Tea from its leaves settles an upset stomach. An infusion of leaves and flowers relieves headaches.
Arroz	Rice	Obatalá	Water in which white rice has been boiled stops diarrhea. Cooked rice meal clears up acne when applied directly on the skin. Eating rice helps maintain a clear complexion.
Boniato, batata	Sweet potato	Oshún, Orishaoko	Its juice, mixed with milk, fortifies bones, brain, and blood.
Cebolla	Onion	All orishas	Onions are natural diuretics. Cooked onions cure insomnia, raw onions prevent the flu and colds.
Canela	Cinnamon	Oshún	Cinnamon tea alleviates intestinal problems; it also cures nausea and stops diarrhea.

TABLE 1. (CONTINUED) HERBS AND THEIR USES IN SANTERIA

Spanish name	English name	Ruling orisha	Medicinal or other uses
Caña de azucar	Sugar cane	Shangó	A tea made from its roots serves as a diuretic. Its juice, mixed with lime and bitter orange juice, fights malaria.
Fruta bomba, lechosa	Papaya	Oyá	When prepared by an experienced osainista, it is said to cure madness.
Manzanilla	Chamomile flowers and leaves	Oshún	Its tea is good for the stomach; it is also a mild sedative. It is good as vaginal or intestinal wash. Washing hair with it prevents dandruff.
Mango	Mango	Oshún	Powder from its seed, mixed with rubbing alcohol, makes an excellent disinfectant.
Maní	Peanut	Babalú Ayé	Aphrodisiac
Marañon	Cashew	Oshún, Inle, Shangó	A string of raw cashews, worn as a belt under clothing, cures hemorrhoids—as the seeds shrivel and fall off, the hemorrhoids shrink.
Maravilla	Witch hazel	Obatalá, Yewa, Oyá	A natural astringent. Tea from the roots cures colic; juice from the whole plant reduces tumors. Rub juice on skin as a mosquito repellent.
Mejorana	Marjoram	Osain, Oshún	Tea eases labor pains.
Yerba buena	Spearmint	Yemayá	Mixed with rum and applied directly to the affected area, it clears up skin conditions like acne.

NOTES

1. Lydia Cabrera, *El Monte*, 6th ed. (Miami: Coleccion del Chichereku, 1986).

2. Nicolas Valentin Angarica, *Manual del orihate, religion lucumi* (Havana, 1955), 22.

3. Cabrera, 58.

CHAPTER 12

CHARADA CHINA

Many people in Cuba and the United States wonder how those who are involved in Santeria, often very poor people, always seem to be able to afford the relatively high cost of initiations. The kariocha initiation, for example, can cost the equivalent of two years' wages for a low-income person. Expensive items associated with kariocha include the animals needed for sacrifice, which are later served at a grandiose feast; the regal robes initiates must wear on the day of their "crowning"; the soup tureens where the sacred stones and other symbols of the orishas are kept; and the fees of the numerous specialists associated with the initiation. Stories of people depriving themselves of all luxuries for years in order to pay for their initiations are common, but more perplexing are stories, also common, of people who pay for their initiations with money won in the lottery or other games of chance, supposedly after an orisha or a guardian spirit revealed to them which numbers to play.

Santeros believe orishas and guardian spirits have the ability, if they so choose, to predict what number will come out in the lottery or what horse will win a race. Spirits and orishas are capricious in this respect, however, and rarely give numbers in a forthright manner. Instead, they give coded clues that require special knowledge to interpret them. This knowledge comes from a surprising source, China.

Between the late 1840s and the early 1870s, an estimated 125,000 Chinese contract laborers were imported to work under indenture in Cuba.[1] As ex-slave Estéban Montejo has noted, they often worked on the same plantations as the African slaves.[2] The Cantonese supposedly brought with them a kind of lottery known in Cuba as *bicho colgado* (hanging bug). The person who ran the game—the *banco*—would write a number from 1 to 36 on a piece of paper and fold it up. The folded paper was hung from a string in the ceiling, where all could see it but not touch or alter it. The banco would give a vague clue to what the number was; knowledge of a code called the *charada* was essential for deciphering the clue. After people had written down their guesses, the banco would lower the piece of paper and announce the number. Depending on the banco, he or she would pay those who had correctly guessed the number either a percentage of the collected revenue or a preset amount.

The *charada* was a full-length portrait of a Chinese man, or *chino*, on whose body tiny figures of people, animals, and objects were drawn (see Figure 3, page 108). Next to each figure, a number was written. If the banco's clue was, for example, "Smaller than a lobster," the answer might be "shrimp," which in the *charada* corresponds to the number 30. Less obvious correspondences are also suggested. Number 30, for example, also represents the male reproductive organ. This is suggested by the position and place of the shrimp on the Chinese man's portrait. Although at first only the Chinese played the game, blacks soon began to play *charada china* and learned the correspondences in the portrait of the soon-to-be-famous *chino*, one of the most reproduced pictures in Cuba. At some point, someone began to notice a purported correspondence among dreams, the *charada,* and winning in games of chance. It seemed that the orishas liked to give numbers using clues from the *charada!* By the early part of the twentieth century, sixty-four more numbers were added to the traditional thirty-six, giving the *charada* an even one hundred numbers. Table 2 lists the one hundred numbers and their most frequently cited correspondences.

FIGURE 3. THE "CHARADA" MANDARIN

TABLE 2. THE CHARADA CHINA CODE

1. horse	34. monkey	68. big cemetery
2. butterfly	35. spider	69. water well
3. sailor	36. pipe	70. coconut
4. cat	37. witchcraft	71. river
5. nun	38. hermit crab	72. train
6. tortoise, turtle	39. small snake	73. park
7. snail, seashell,	40. Catholic priest	74. kite
excrement	41. lizard	75. movie
8. death	42. duck	76. ballerina, dancer
9. elephant	43. scorpion	77. flags
10. big fish	44. leather	78. bishop
11. rooster	45. shark, president	79. fancy car
12. saintly woman,	46. smoke	80. physician
whore	47. bird, homosexual	81. theater
13. peacock, pimp	man	82. lion
14. tiger, striped cat	48. cockroach	83. tragedy
15. dog	49. drunk	84. tailor
16. bull	50. policeman	85. Madrid
17. moon	51. private 1st class	86. convent
18. small fish	52. bicycle	87. New York
19. earthworm	53. electric light	88. eyeglasses
20. fancy cat	54. white hen	89. lottery
21. big snake	55. crab	90. large mirror, old
22. toad, frog	56. queen	man
23. steamship	57. telegram	91. streetcar
24. dove	58. adultery	92. balloon
25. gemstone	59. phonograph	93. revolution
26. eel	60. dark sun	94. machete
27. wasp	61. cannon shot	95. war
28. goat, anus, vagina	62. marriage	96. challenge
29. mouse	63. murderer	97. large mosquito
30. shrimp, penis	64. gunshot	98. piano
31. deer	65. jail	99. coal vendor
32. pig	66. divorce	100. inn, motel
33. vulture	67. stabbing	

Believers interpret not only dreams but also other unusual occurrences according to the *charada*. If, for example, someone is bitten by a dog, he or she might play number 15 that day. Santeros also added to the *charada* the emblematic numbers of the orishas (Shangó—4; Oyá—9; Oshún—5, and so forth). Some of the numbers have African, some Catholic symbolism. Because of the variety of meanings possible and the apparently convoluted way the orishas chose to communicate winning numbers, it sometimes requires the sagacity of a Sherlock Holmes to decipher a dream or event. A santera in Puerto Rico recently won a lottery using the following approach:

> I dreamt my father was giving my ex-husband a statue of Saint Lazarus. Well, Saint Lazarus' feast day is the seventeenth of December; my father is dead—number 8—and he was a sailor—number 3. I always chided my husband about his . . . well, he was overly endowed, so I played number 30. 17, 8, 3, 30. Bingo! I won enough money to undergo the Babalú Ayé initiation I so desperately needed.

Sometimes a source of merriment, the *charada* is also taken seriously in Santeria as a way chosen by the orishas to communicate winning numbers. The adoption of the Chinese *charada* by Afro-Cubans again demonstrates their capacity for adapting foreign ideas to their specific needs without compromising their identity and origins.

——————————— NOTES ———————————

1. Louis A. Perez, *Cuba: Between Reform and Revolution* (New York: Oxford University Press, 1988), 115.

2. Miguel Barnet, *Biografia de un cimarron* [Autobiography of a Runaway Slave] (Barcelona: Ediciones Ariel, 1968), 24.

CHAPTER 13

THE DARK SIDE OF SANTERIA

Any system that practices manipulation of power offers a temptation for the unprincipled and greedy to misuse that power. Unfortunately, some people abuse the spiritual power of Santeria in a number of ways, including bringing about harm to individuals for revenge or personal gain. While not publicized as much as animal sacrifice, this issue is, in my opinion, more damaging to Santeria's reputation: that people who have been chosen by the orishas to channel their power misuse this gift for petty, personal aims.

Many santeros who use their powers to work evil do so not under the guise of Santeria but of Palo. Among Afro-Cubans, while Santeria

is considered a religion of devotion to the higher powers, Palo has
been equated with "workings," or magic. A religion that evolved
among the descendants of the Congo peoples who were brought to
Cuba, Palo exhibits a good/evil duality that does not exist in
Santeria; a *palero* will deliberately choose to do evil, whereas the
actions of a santero may have an unfortunate outcome but are
carried out with the intention of balancing ashé. Because Palo uses
human remains in its rituals, many santeros feel it is very important
to disassociate Santeria from Palo.

Despite these differences and the disdain in which many Yoruba-
descended Lucumís hold the Congo heritage of the paleros, some
santeros will readily patronize a palero in order to get results. An
old santera in Miami once told me,

> Getting results with Santeria is almost as slow as getting
> results with the [Catholic] Church; you ask your saint for
> things and you wait for him to help you. In Palo, those
> *gangás*[1] are like slaves, they'll do whatever the palero
> tells them. . . . If you want to feel good, you worship the
> orishas. If you want something done, you go to a palero.

Palo cannot be blamed for all evil workings in Santeria, but it should
be kept in mind as an influence.

Speaking with several members of my family who were or con-
tinue to be santeros while researching the material for this book,
I came across one of the most moving stories to be included here.
It happened to a cousin of mine who is now an elder in the Jehovah's
Witnesses. I wanted to know why he had not only left Santeria but
became an outspoken enemy of the religion. His story shows what
I would call the dark side of the religion.

Years ago when we were both around ten years old, my cousin's
mother had inherited $32,000—a small fortune for her—and had
managed to smuggle the money out of communist Cuba with her
husband, my cousin's stepfather. He planned to use the money to
start a business in the United States and send for my cousin and
his mother once he was established. In Miami, the stepfather, Pepe

(not his real name), met with an old acquaintance, a woman who had owned several dingy nightclubs in Havana and now owned a dilapidated but large and promising bar in Miami. The woman (whom we'll call Lola) offered Pepe a fifty-fifty partnership in her bar if he would invest his $32,000 and his expertise (he had been a nightclub manager in Havana) in making something of her bar.

With singleness of purpose, Pepe threw himself to the task of renovating Lola's place. In a few weeks, the sparkling new nightclub opened to rave reviews and splendid crowds. Pepe couldn't have been happier—his hard work and wise investment was going to pay off! A friend from Havana who had been a lawyer back in Cuba asked Pepe if his partnership with Lola was in writing. Pepe, who had handled other people's money as a trusted manager since the age of fifteen without ever having signed a contract, thought that among Cubans such formalities were unnecessary; Lola had said fifty-fifty, and that was that. Worried, Pepe's friend told him that in the United States such verbal contracts were useless and that he should ask Lola to draw up a written contract.

Pepe good-naturedly brought the subject of the contract up with Lola. She laughed at him and told him that he owned nothing; the nightclub was all hers. She then ordered her bouncers to forcefully evict Pepe from the premises and later took out a restraining order against Pepe forbidding him to come within one hundred feet of the club. In this way Pepe found himself penniless and hungry in the streets of Miami. In Havana my cousin's mother went to see our madrina, Amanda, seeking revenge, but Amanda advised her to let Lola's actions create her own doom; the powers of the orishas were not to be used to harm others, even if they deserved it. At the time my cousin was staying with Amanda in order to learn *ocha*, the way of the orishas. Seeing his mother devastated, dejected, and frustrated at Amanda's unwillingness to help her, he too felt sad and frustrated and wished he could do something.

In a little hut behind Amanda's house, partially hidden in the bush, lived an ancient lady, Amanda's grandmother. All the children feared this strange creature who never spoke and only emerged from her mysterious abode to empty her chamber pot. She was a wizened old woman who had celebrated her centennial an improbable number of years back. Her eyes were filmed over a light blue, without iris or pupil, from her great age. My cousin was sitting behind Amanda's house when the old woman spoke to him. Using the rarely heard Bozal dialect, she said, "Yo se que pasa con tu, si tu ta beni mi baraco, yo tu 'yuda" (I know what is wrong with you, come inside my house and I'll help you). When he entered the hut, my cousin was surprised at how clean and orderly everything was; the smell of newly ironed sheets gave the whole place a very fresh feeling. Continuing to speak in Bozal—which most Cubans understand because it forms part of traditional theater even though it is rarely spoken in real life in the twentieth century—the old woman told my cousin that she was aware of what had happened to his mother and stepfather and if he wanted, he could help them.

"The Ibeyi are very powerful, they are two little children, the sons of Shangó and Oyá. If you and your little brother do as I say, that evil *panchágara* [whore] who stole your mother's life savings will pay." My cousin told the old woman he would do whatever she told him. "First, we need some personal effects from her, otherwise there's nothing we can do." He explained the difficulty of obtaining personal effects from a person in Miami, but she insisted that if he could not get that, there was nothing she could do. The next day, however, he was amazed to discover that, before she had broken with Pepe, Lola had sent my cousin's mother a package of used blouses, underwear, and other articles of clothing, most of them not even laundered. He picked out a particularly worn bra that seemed not to have been washed and gave it to the old woman in the hut. Taking some black cloth, some hairlike roots, and other powders and herbs, singing softly, the old woman fashioned a doll out of the black cloth, putting pieces of the bra, black candle wax, and the other ingredients inside the doll, which she then sewed up. Out of other pieces of the bra the old woman fashioned a head scarf and a little dress for the doll. "Call your little brother over here," the old woman said to my cousin. When he came in, the old woman made them both prostrate themselves in front of a wooden likeness of the Ibeyi, the twin orishas, while she recited a long prayer in Lucumí.

"Make a little cardboard coffin for Lola," the old woman told my cousin. "You mean the doll?" he asked. Grabbing him by the shoulder with incredible force, the old woman, visibly upset, said, "Listen, *muchachito*, if you want this to work, you must never refer to Lola as a doll. This is Lola, the bitch we are going to send to the other side." Calming down, the old woman slowly repeated her instructions: "Make a little cardboard coffin and hold it down with twenty-one straight pins. Put three straight pins into Lola in places where it would normally kill a person—her heart and brain, for example. Later, light a nine-day black candle and you and your little brother must cry over Lola for nine days, at the end of which you must bury her outside the cemetery but not in consecrated ground."

Children can be more resourceful than adults will believe, for the two boys did as they were told without anyone in their household finding out. The curse was supposed to work in twenty-one days, so when twenty-five days passed by and no news of anything happening to Lola reached us, my cousin figured that either the old lady was lying or they didn't do things correctly. At the end of thirty days, however, they found out Lola had been murdered earlier that morning by a Haitian she had bamboozled just as she had Pepe.

For years my cousin said he felt guilty about the death of Lola. As an adult he finally met a wonderful psychiatrist who also knew a lot about Santeria; he helped my cousin resolve that conflict by pointing out that Lola's death was not a consequence of his curse. The psychiatrist told him, "I am acquainted with that particular curse. It works in nine days, twenty-one days, or not at all. It never works in thirty days. Besides, that curse only works on people who really deserve it. That evil woman just had her come-uppance from her own actions. I'm surprised she didn't get it sooner." The psychiatrist helped him regain some clarity, but my cousin rejected Santeria completely. He turned to the Jehovah's Witnesses, whom he claims helped him feel whole again.

Hearing my cousin's story helped me understand his conversion to a religion so different from the one we both had grown up in. As he spoke, I remembered Lola's mysterious death and how at about that time my cousin had begun to require professional counseling. I did not have the heart to tell him, however, that that particular spell does not require a specific time period and that thirty days is a very common period of time for such spells to take effect.

A while ago I experienced a similar incident, this time clearly with Palo overtones. While conducting my research on Palo's relationship to Santeria, quite by accident I came across an altar that featured the photograph of a dear friend in a position I recognized as being meant to cause him great harm. The Santeria/Palo practitioners in question had no knowledge of my friendship with this person. I became extremely anxious—what was I to do? These people had welcomed me into their homes in order to help my research, but at the same time I had been around Santeria too long not to know that what they were doing to my friend could cause his death. In fact, I had recently noticed that his state of mind had deteriorated considerably. Knowing I was breaking a scholar's oath not to interfere with his subjects, I nevertheless used a tactic that could have caused my death. When the people weren't looking, I took the fundamental cowrie shells that contain the ashé of the orisha out of the soup tureen that my friend's photograph stood before, thus rendering the spell powerless. In the next few days, my friend's health began to improve. Fortunately I suffered no ill effects—there was a possibility that the spirit in the tureen could have killed me. I hope I am never again in a situation where I have to make such a choice.

While greed and self-interest are not U.S. monopolies, I sometimes wonder how the American focus on the material plane has affected Santeria and santeros in this country. In New Orleans, in 1972, I was undergoing a period of apprenticeship with my friend Ifá P. (not his real name), at the time the only babalao in the state of Louisiana. One day La Mora, the senior santera of the area, came excitedly to my house to tell me that a new babalao had just arrived from Los Angeles. I went to see this new babalao and discovered that he was somehow related to me—his daughter was married to my grandmother's cousin's son. In my family, relationships so tenuous that Americans would consider them inconsequential are deemed sacred, so after establishing that the new babalao was a cousin, I did as I was expected and invited him to stay in my house. To my surprise, Paco Cuevas turned out to be a man of amazing wisdom, an unforgettable character from whom I was to learn much. Paco had been run out of Los Angeles by the Santeria community there because he was against keeping Santeria's secrets. Paco would reveal the most closely guarded secrets to anyone, saying that in Africa that was the way the religion was carried out—in the open. At first Ifá P. welcomed Paco but he soon became jealous, for Paco, an older babalao, simply knew more and began to attract clients away from Ifá P.

One day Ifá P. demanded that I spy on Paco for him, saying that Padrino had named him my sponsor in the United States and I owed my allegiance to him. I told Ifá P. that I could not do that because Paco was a relative; besides, I didn't think our padrino back in Havana would approve of such tactics. Ifá P. became visibly upset and said, "I've had enough of Paco Cuevas." With that, he stormed out of my house.

Paco had rented a beautiful apartment on Elysian Fields, across the street from my house. That night was oppressively hot and I could not sleep, so I sat by my bedroom window watching the scene outside. At around midnight, I clearly saw Ifá P.'s car slow down in front of Paco's place for a moment and then rush off.

Early the next morning, an agitated Paco came to my door saying that he had to leave New Orleans immediately. I tried to reason with him but he refused to heed my counsel. He took the first bus to Miami, leaving behind most of his belongings and a thriving practice. Years later I was to hear through the grapevine that what Ifá P. had done that night was to blow ground Angola pepper on Paco's door, probably reinforced with stronger ingredients. This practice creates a spell that makes people want to flee. Paco, a truly good person, had not been prepared to deal with such pettiness. When I learned this I lost all respect for Ifá P. and diplomatically ended my apprenticeship with him. Paco Cuevas later moved back to Los Angeles, where he lived for many years.

With incidents like this, on the one hand I am amazed that the force of the supernatural survives in Santeria in the United States. On the other, I wonder: would this have taken place between two babalaos back in Cuba?

The following story illustrates a different shade of Santeria's dark side, one tinted as much by the colors of ignorance as of greed. As has been mentioned earlier, the process of "making saint" in the United States is often condensed from three years to as many months. This can lead not only to a lack of understanding and to syncretic practices but to new santeros trying to be what they are not. In their quest for legitimacy, these people are often taken advantage of by established santeros, who see them as a source of easy money. I attended one bembé a few years ago that was a pathetic example of this.

Jimmy, an Anglo *omo* Shangó, was holding the bembé to celebrate his seventh year *en santo.* He had been initiated in New York by a highly esteemed Puerto Rican santera, Asunta Serrano, and in both New York and Miami he had tried to be accepted as an equal by the Cuban Santeria community without success. Since moving to an out-of-the-way farm near Tampa two years before, Jimmy had courted Tampa santeros, but for the most part they considered him a curiosity because he was Anglo.

While the really important santeros—the ones with the most godchildren—shunned Jimmy's bembé, enough Cubans showed up to make him wild with excitement. When I arrived, however, I noticed a few things that did not bode well for the bembé's success. For one thing, rather than hire a recognized, initiated batá ensemble, he had hired a group with roots in Santeria but whose style is probably closer to standard Yoruba than to Lucumí. The food he was offering, too, was not what Afro-Cubans consider standard fare at a bembé—spinach quiche and celery stalks.

As the musicians played, Jimmy tried desperately to have orishas possess the people, who were dancing and doing their best. Jimmy furiously rang Obatalá's silver bell over people who belonged to Obatalá's priesthood, a tactic thought to speed up the possession. Finally a friend of Jimmy's, a nineteen-year-old Puerto Rican who claims he was initiated in Miami, fell to the floor dramatically. Another santera of dubious reputation—sources in Cuba say she was never initiated—also fell. Jimmy was ecstatic—two orishas came to his party! The santera, supposedly possessed by Yemayá, saluted Jimmy's friend's Obatalá. As if trying to convince himself, Jimmy wildly shouted, "Look, everyone, Yemayá is saluting Regis' Obatalá. That means his possession is real!"

A heavyset man in his fifties took me by the arm and led me outside. He was Balu, a santero-palero who works mainly with Palo and is extremely respected in Tampa, where he has a hundred godchildren. I had never met Balu before but somehow I knew who he was, just as he knew who I was. He removed his dark glasses and looked straight into my eyes. Without saying a word, I knew exactly what he was thinking. Not knowing what to do, I said, "Yemayá did salute him, isn't that a sign of . . ." Balu did not let me finish: "Tweedle-Dum certifying Tweedle-Dummer." I couldn't help laughing.

Jimmy values my opinion highly; he considers me in some way vital to his eventual acceptance by the Cubans—an acceptance that he craves. I felt sorry for him because he had been so nice to me. I thought about recommending that he contact Omi Dina in Tampa, an American santero who has little use for Cubans in his ilé and yet is recognized as legitimate. I also tried to make Jimmy understand that he could be a santero without having to kowtow to any one group, that Santeria was becoming international.

After most people had left the bembé, Jimmy asked for my opinion. He asked me whether, as a priest of Obatalá, I was not moved by the visit the great orisha had paid us through Regis. Perhaps because of the lateness of the hour and how tired I was, I found myself juxtaposing in my mind the image of Amanda—totally transfixed, her facial features transformed and her voice other-worldly as Obatalá spoke through her—with the pitiful image of Regis, his eyes closed, trying to sound African, talking nonsense to the people. Trying to be diplomatic, I told Jimmy that perhaps Regis had felt Obatalá so close that he believed himself possessed, but that I did not think what we had seen that night was an actual case of orisha possession. Becoming defensive, Jimmy said, "But the santera's Yemayá saluted Regis' Obatalá!" I replied, "What makes you think she was really possessed? Don't you know that in Tampa she is considered a phony?"

A week after Jimmy's bembé, I received a letter from him telling me how hurt he was that I had not recognized his friend's orisha possession but that Balu, the respected santero-palero, was going to publicly give his blessing to Regis, announcing that the possession had indeed been real. Jimmy also mentioned in the letter that the announcement was to take place at a bembé given at Balu's house in honor of Regis' Obatalá, for which he was only charging Regis $7,000.

I had no idea what Regis and Jimmy would get in exchange for their $7,000, but I was in no mood to find out. I decided not to go to Balu's bembé. Instead, I would stay home, close my eyes, and remember Amanda, Mantilla, and a magical night long ago in a land of endless summers and refreshing rainfalls, a land perhaps now existing only in my dreams, a land of orishas, a land of beauty, a land of honesty. . . .

---------------------------- NOTES ----------------------------

1. *Gangá* is Palero's cauldron, including the human remains within it.

CHAPTER 14

SANTERIA:
WORLD RELIGION?

Santeria is growing in the United States beyond its traditional ethnic boundaries. Numerous African Americans, non-Hispanic West Indians, and European Americans are embracing Santeria. The advent of non-Cubans to this traditionally Afro-Cuban religion is bringing about the transformation of a religion that was in many ways primal to one that can be characterized as universal in scope. What this change in the ethnic makeup of participants, from exclusively Cuban and Puerto Rican to increasingly multiethnic and non-Hispanic, will mean to Santeria in the United States is hard to predict, but it is obviously an important development that deserves close scrutiny.

Santeria or the Lucumí religion in Cuba was at first open only to African-born Yorubas. Later, non-Yoruba Africans were admitted, followed by Afro-Cubans and eventually whites. I have heard anecdotal stories of santeros migrating to Puerto Rico in the first half of the nineteenth century. Migene González-Wippler, a Puerto Rican who has written on Santeria and is a professed believer, states that she first encountered Santeria when she was five years old through a black Puerto Rican servant who had been initiated by a Cuban immigrant.[1]

Although many sources name Francisco (Pancho) Mora as the first santero in the United States (he moved from Cuba to New York in 1946), I have found documentary evidence indicating that by 1939 Afro-Cuban religious groups were operating in Ybor City, now part of Tampa, Florida.[2] Mercedes, an African American woman in her forties, has told me that her great-grandparents who moved from Cuba to Ybor City in 1876 were santeros, as must have been some of the thousands of Afro-Cubans who came to work in the cigar factories of Tampa and Key West during the last decades of the nineteenth century. Santeria's strict rule of secrecy must have been intensified in the antiblack, Protestant mentality of the southern United States at that time. Even today, descendants of those nineteenth-century Afro-Cuban cigar workers are among the most secretive santeros I have ever encountered.

The first documented case of a non-Hispanic American being initiated as a santero is Walter King, an African American who was initiated in Cuba in 1959.[3] King, who later changed his name to Oba Osejiman Adefumi I, became a well-known figure in the black power movement of the 1960s, infusing his interpretation of Santeria with elements of black pride. He now heads a Yoruba revitalization movement headquartered in Oyotunji Village, South Carolina. Several thousand people, mostly African Americans, follow Adefumi's teachings. Although Adefumi has formally broken with Cuban Santeria, his movement by definition depends on it for legitimacy and continuity. The first white American initiated into Santeria about whom we have clear documentation—as opposed to anecdotal references—is the noted anthropologist Judith Gleason. Gleason was initiated in New York City by the Puerto Rican santera Asunta Serrano around 1963.

Santeria, with its overwhelming demonstration of African retentions, is understandably appealing to people of African descent, such as African Americans and black West Indians. These groups appear to be, in fact, the fastest-growing among non-Hispanic newcomers to Santeria.[4] White, non-Hispanic, American santeros, however, appear to be on the rise. One of the ilés I studied, located in southern Florida, is headed by a well-educated white American couple who leads a multiethnic group including Hispanics, African Americans, and whites. This ilé is unusual in that most of the people associated with it are well educated and relatively affluent, in contrast to Santeria's traditional identification with the lower classes.

An article in *New York Magazine* on October 12, 1987 examined the growing phenomenon of whites becoming involved in Santeria. It mentions several celebrities who have publicly expressed interest in the religion, among them the late artist Keith Haring, Judith Gleason, and the drummer John Amira. Amira is quoted as saying, "I came into Santeria from pop music, an area that had nothing to do with this. I was drawn into it—I got involved in ceremonial music and finally in the religion itself."[5] In the Latin music world, musicians such as Tito Puente and Chano Pozo have long been associated with Santeria, not surprising when one considers the enormous importance of drum beats and African rhythmic patterns in the religion. More recently, pop musicians David Byrne and Paul Simon independently have recorded music heavily influenced by Candonblé, the Brazilian counterpart of Santeria.

The incursion of non-Hispanics into Santeria can also be observed in formerly all-Cuban ilés. I have followed the development of Ifá P.'s ilé since his arrival from Cuba in 1972. A babalao, Ifá P. was welcomed by the small Santeria community in New Orleans since, at that time, there were no other babalaos in the area. By 1973, his ilé consisted of two hundred people from Louisiana and neighboring states; they were all Cubans. In 1974 Ifá P. moved to Miami, where he prospered. He claimed to have a thousand "godchildren" (a sign of success in Santeria), nine hundred of whom were Cubans, the rest Puerto Ricans and Colombians.[6] By 1990, Ifá P.'s ilé had grown to five thousand members who were spread throughout the United States and South and Central America. Surprisingly, Ifá P. says that now 60 percent of his "godchildren" are non-Hispanics; of these, he says 50 percent are African Americans, 25 percent are blacks from the Caribbean (mostly Haitians and Jamaicans), and the rest are whites.

Ifá P. claims that negative media attention has sparked some people's interest in Santeria, leading some to investigate the religion and then become involved with it. An apparent general upsurge of interest in nontraditional religious expressions, often grouped together as New Age philosophies, may have also contributed to the increased interest in Santeria. Ifá P. says most of his non-Hispanic followers have joined his ilé in the last five years. Cary, proprietor of one of the many *botánicas*[7] found in West Tampa, tells me that during the last two years, the number of "Anglos" and African Americans who come to her shop has grown at an exponential rate. She also mentions that most of them appear to be very knowledgeable about Santeria.

One of the results of this incursion of non-Hispanics into Santeria is that the long-standing Santeria code of secrecy is being called into question. People who have grown up with the idea that religious freedom is an inalienable right do not see any reason to hide their adherence to an ancient religion that is not intrinsically "worse" than others. African American santeros especially appear to want to proclaim their allegiance to Santeria, many of them prominently displaying the multicolored necklaces that identify them as believers. In the upper-middle-class ilé described earlier, members see Santeria as an instrument through which certain dimensions of the "cosmic mind" not easily reached can be accessed; they have discarded many aspects of traditional Cuban Santeria, such as not discussing the religion with outsiders, as obsolete. Another aspect that is being abandoned, even by some Cuban-led ilés, is the virtual paranoia most Cuban santeros and practitioners constantly experience as a result of believing that, if they are not careful, they could fall victims to curses and poisons. While traditional santeros will not eat or drink outside of their homes, will not allow their heads to be touched, and try not to have their photographs taken, the more progressive ilés reflect the relative openness of American society; their members enjoy considerably greater camaraderie without having to be constantly on guard.

The considerable number of non-Cubans who are joining the ranks of Santeria has resulted in the religion losing some of its ethnocentric, cliquish character. Purists consider Cuban geography and other aspects of Cuban culture, such as the use of Spanish in certain rituals and Santeria's relationship to the especially intense Hispanic form of Catholicism, indispensable to the religion. Santeria priests like the late babalao Pancho Mora do not recognize "Made in the USA" babalaos, stating that high priests can only be consecrated on Cuban soil. Their reasoning is that powerful stones, or Olofi artifacts, brought from Africa are needed for babalao consecrations, and these stones have supposedly never left Cuba. However, Ifa P. told me that he saw one Olofi artifact with his own eyes in the home of famous Miami babalao Carlos Ojeda, who must have brought it from Cuba. Non-Cubans correctly point out that Cuban geography cannot be so essential since the religion was originally taken to Cuba from Africa. They argue that since the religion survived the Middle Passage, adapting to the Cuban environment, it can also survive the trek across the Florida straits and adapt to the American environment.

One result of a Santeria devoid of dependency on Cuban geography and customs might be its transformation from a basically localized primal religion, dependent on Cuban soil, to an essentially universal religion expression (albeit with an obvious African flavor) that encompasses all who will enter. Secrecy would be left behind as anachronistic.

Although the increasing numbers of non-Hispanics in American Santeria—and the subsequent transformation of the religion—has received scant attention, I believe this phenomenon needs to be scrutinized. Never before has a religion that is based on a sub-Saharan African tradition, the Yoruba, gained so many converts in

the United States—African Americans, West Indians, and, significantly, European Americans. I hope that the recognition of this
trend will spark widespread interest and lead to better understanding of this potentially important development, one pregnant with
possibilities for meaningful research.

The 1990s are ushering a new wave of Western seekers, as well
as a reawakening of the spirit of peoples of non-Western traditions
who are discovering the strength of their own traditions and re-
asserting the original potency of their religious practices. Let us
hope that, learning from the past, such seekers will strive to avoid
the pitfalls of power and will use these ancient traditions not for
selfish ends but for the good of humankind.

NOTES

1. Migene González-Wippler, *Santeria, the Religion* (New York: Harmony Books, 1989), 291-304.

2. Manuel Marrero, "The Ñáñigo Cult in Ybor City," unpublished paper
written for the WPA's Writers' Project, 1939 (Special Collections
Department, University of South Florida, Tampa).

3. Steven Gregory, *Santeria in New York City: A Study in Cultural
Resistance,* Ph.D. diss., New School for Social Research, 1986, 62-65.

4. Ibid., 1-2.

5. Tracy Cochran, "Among the Believers: Converts to Santeria," *New
York Magazine,* October 12, 1987, 33-34.

6. A number of santeros have informed me that many Colombians in
the narcotics underground seek supernatural help in Santeria as a
protection against the authorities. One santero has told me that he
only "pretends" to give the drug smugglers protection: "My santos won't
let me give protection to such people, but I'll take their money and
give them worthless amulets anytime I can." I find it interesting that
drug smugglers may often be victims of fraud in Santeria.

7. *Botánicas* are shops specializing in Santeria paraphernalia. The
name refers to the many herbs and plants sold at these stores. *Botánicas*
often serve as gathering places and clearinghouses for believers.

APPENDIX

BLACKS IN CUBA:
AN OVERVIEW

> Before Castro, our island was a racial paradise where
> Cubans of every shade joyfully celebrated together, arm
> in arm, the bountiful fruits of their privileged land . . .
> *"La Cuba de ayer,"* television documentary, 1966

The above statement, from a popular feature-length documentary
produced by Cuban exiles in the United States, formulates a sentiment often expressed by Cubans. In Tampa, Florida, I was recently
invited to participate in a radio call-in program on racism. I was
mercilessly assailed by many callers because I challenged the myth
of Cuban color blindness. Interestingly, all of the callers who identified themselves as white strongly objected to the contention that
racism has had a long history in Cuba, while all who said they were

"colored" (a term still employed by Cubans) stated that they had suffered racial discrimination from fellow Cubans.

Another panelist in the program, a Cuban-born university professor, agreed with me that there has been racism among Cubans, but he believes that such sentiments were learned from the United States during the period of American influence in Cuba (1898-1959). I propose that racism was an integral part of Cuban society long before the United States became heavily involved with the island; furthermore, Cuban racism exhibits certain idiosyncrasies that distinguish it from what we will call the southern U.S. model.

In America, any individual who has a known Negro ancestor is considered black, and the black race constitutes a single subordinate group, or "caste." This so-called "one-drop-makes-a-whole" rule is not found in Cuban racism—only the titled aristocracy pays serious attention to pedigree. In Cuba, racial typing follows a more complex and subtle system, based on gradations of color and physical characteristics, along a continuum from "pure white" (most desirable) to "pure black" (least desirable).[1] Race relations strongly influenced the development of Santeria in Cuba; to understand Santeria it is important to understand the black-white dynamics of Cuban society.

Large-scale slavery was introduced to Cuba at a relatively late date compared to other parts of the New World. The first African slaves were brought to Cuba in 1501 to replace the rapidly dwindling indigenous population, which had been decimated by the Spaniards.[2] In 1639 Pope Urban VIII denounced slavery and issued a bull condemning slave trafficking and forbidding Catholics from engaging in "that abominable enterprise."[3] In 1683 the Spanish crown issued an edict stating that "slave traffickers are to be prosecuted and punished severely."[4] Because of these factors slavery in Cuba was practiced on a small scale prior to the eighteenth century, and slaves who labored on the island led relatively easy lives compared to other slaves in the non-Spanish Caribbean and the American South.

In 1713, however, the treaty of Utrecht reversed that trend by granting the new superpower, Britain, the right to sell slaves in the Spanish colonies. When the British occupied Havana Harbor in 1762 during the Seven Years' War, they imported massive numbers of slaves from Africa. Although the English stayed for only one year, the economic consequences of their victory forever transformed Cuban society. Once a Spanish monopoly, Cuban trade was opened by the British to the rest of Europe.

By the second half of the eighteenth century, sugar consumption in Europe had grown at an exponential rate. To satisfy the enormous sweet tooth that had erupted in Europe, Cuba was transformed from a small-scale producer of sugar, tobacco, and cattle to the world's largest sugarcane field. As David Booth points out: "The lateness of the apogee of plantation Slavery in Cuba had numerous decisive consequences for the type of socio-racial structure that emerged in the twentieth century."[5]

By the dawn of the nineteenth century, British sentiments had turned decidedly against slavery. As C. Stanley Urban writes:

> England and France placed pressure on Spain to abolish slavery in Cuba and to substitute it with a system of free labor; these demands gave rise to a great deal of social and political tensions on the island.[6]

However, fear of economic instability and revolution prevented the abolition of slavery until 1880.

After the triumph of the 1804 slave revolt in Saint Domingue, Cuba's closest neighbor, numerous white and mulatto planters fled the newly created black nation of Haiti and sought refuge in Cuba. Their tales of horror fueled the Cuban planters' fears of a black uprising. Dread of the *peligro negro* (black menace) reached hysterical proportions in Cuba during the first half of the nineteenth century. Several scholars, including Robert L. Paquette, have suggested that fear of nonwhite dominance may have delayed Cuban independence by at least fifty years. In 1836 the Spanish minister, Calatrava, could accurately boast to the U.S. ambassador to Spain Cornelius Van Ness, "Fear of the Negro is worth an army of 100,000 men; it will prevent whites [in Cuba] from making any revolutionary attempts."[7] In the early 1840s a group of enlightened white and colored creoles led a conspiracy against the colonial power in what has come to be known as the "La Escalera" revolt. The rebels were aided by the British consul in Havana, David Turnbull, who was later tried and convicted in absentia as the "prime mover behind La Escalera." One of the reasons the movement may not have received widespread support may have been that its most visible leader, the poet Placido, was a mulatto; Placido was hanged by the Spanish authorities.[8]

By the middle of the nineteenth century, U.S. expansionism and white Cuba's fears of the *peligro negro* converged, resulting in an upsurge of proannexation sentiment in both nations. President Franklin Pierce of the United States tried to pressure Spain into selling Cuba to his country, a move that was probably supported by a majority of the white planters in Cuba. In the 1840s and 1850s, the majority of white Cuban planters were vociferously proslavery and pro-South. President Pierce would have had to face the problem of Cuba wanting to be admitted to the Union as a slave state! This affinity of nineteenth-century Cubans for southern whites is ironic in light of the fact that in the 1960s many Cubans suffered discrimination in certain parts of the South when they settled there as political exiles.

It needs to be pointed out, however, that even at the height of the *peligro negro* scare, Cuban racial relations were not as bifurcated as in the United States—Placido himself had been received in Cuba's most exclusive parlors. An American southerner observed in 1846:

> Spanish courtesy throws a certain veil over the features of the children of Afric[*sic*]. One, here, has so often to meet on an equal footing with those who are not of pure blood, even in the best society, that our Southern feelings, for the time being, are thrown aside, and we play the Spaniard in his universal politeness.[9]

In Cuba, a rich black or mulatto was more likely to be received in good society than a poor white. Another feature of Cuban racial attitudes is that, while aristocrats might pay attention to a person's pedigree, a person who looks phenotypically white is generally treated as white, regardless of ancestry. In other words, a black in Cuba can have white descendants. This is the reason for the (by U.S. standards) highly inflated "70 percent white" figures usually listed on demographic reports, which many Cubans point out with pride when they state that "Cuba is the whitest of the Caribbean islands." With tongue only slightly in cheek I can say that if the "one-drop-makes-a-whole" rule were applied in Cuba, the country would be as black as Nigeria.

By 1868, when the first massive attempt to overthrow Spanish colonialism erupted, Cuban nationalism finally coalesced. Carlos Manuel de Cespedes, the great Cuban who led the revolt, freed all his slaves so that they could fight for their land as free men and women. Cespedes, a white planter, was not totally freed from racial prejudices, however. He is known to have asked the United States for assurances that, in the event of the fall of Spain, blacks would not be permitted to take over the island as they had done in Haiti.[10] And the brilliant mulatto general Antonio Maceo, the outstanding tactician of Cuba's wars of independence, was forced to complain to Cespedes, president of the "republic-in-arms," about the rampant racism black soldiers were experiencing from the white officers of the revolutionary army.[11] During the Ten Years' War (1868-1878) a large number of incredibly gifted black and mulatto leaders emerged, ushering in, at least superficially, a period of racial harmony—especially among intellectuals. One of the most gifted of the nonwhite revolutionary leaders was the remarkable Juan Gualberto Gomez (1854-1935).

Juan Gualberto's slave parents purchased his freedom before he was born.[12] He was educated in Paris, where many people of African descent had found an amiable environment. Juan Gualberto's impressive record has been trivialized by Cuban historians in the single line "he was a good friend of our apostle, José Marti," but he was an influential patriot, writer, and civil rights leader.

In 1889 Spain's supreme tribunal decreed that no public place had the right to deny any person access because of that person's race or ethnicity. Wanting to test the strength of the court's decision, Juan Gualberto Gomez staged what may have been the first prointegration act of nonviolent civil disobedience in the Americas. Gathering some of the most prominent colored citizens of Havana, Juan Gualberto instructed them to dress in their finest clothes and purchase tickets for the orchestra and mezzanine sections of the Teatro Payret, which were reserved for whites. By custom only the uppermost gallery, the section of the theater derisively known as *la cazuela* (the boiling pot), was open to nonwhites. When the colored patrons refused to be seated in la cazuela, demanding that their tickets be honored, they were arrested for disturbing the peace. Juan Gualberto showed up at police headquarters and demanded that the men and women be freed and the management of the theater be charged with breaking the law, since according to the Spanish tribunal's decision, the people had a right to whatever seats they chose and could afford. The theater relented, and racial segregation in Havana's public places virtually came to an end (it was to be revived years later in American-operated clubs and beaches).[13]

Although Havana and some of the larger cities, such as Santiago, were relatively free of overt, socially condoned racism in public places, the interior of the republic—paradoxically, those places where Americans had the least influence—continued to manifest racial segregation in such places as schools, public parks, and nightclubs. The first white Cuban of note to take an academic interest in Cuba's rich African heritage was the anthropologist Fernando Ortiz. His 1906 work *Los negros brujos* [Negro Witchcraft] ushered in the era of *negrismo* in Cuba. *Negrismo*, closely linked to the *négritude* movement of the francophone islands, saw an eruption of Afro-Cuban art forms reach an international audience. Unfortunately, the success of *negrismo* did not filter down to the colored masses, and it remained an elitist movement.

Realizing that whites were not interested in the betterment of the colored race, black leader Evaristo Estenoz founded the *Partido Independiente de Color*. This unique expression of black Cuban pride was brutally suppressed in what must have been one of Cuba's darkest hours. Booth writes:

In 1912 the brief life of this unique formation was brought to an end when an alleged "black uprising" led by the party's leader, Evaristo Estenoz, was suppressed by government forces amid bloody scenes not unreminiscent of events in the United States in that same period—and not without encouragement from that quarter.[14]

More than three thousand blacks were murdered by hysterical mobs of whites, and the word *lynchar* entered the Cuban lexicon; the "Strange Fruit" Billie Holiday would sing about (lynched blacks hanging from trees) had been exported to Cuba.

In 1933 a colored sergeant named Fulgencio Batista led a revolt of noncommissioned officers against the hated dictator Gerardo Machado, establishing himself as president. Batista's successful coup put a colored man at the head of Cuban affairs for the first time. Although much has been said about Batista's connections to American gangsters and his often ruthless and corrupt regime, his positive achievements, especially concerning blacks and mulattos, have been largely ignored. Although Batista was a light-skinned mulatto, in Cuba's complex system of racial classification he could not quite make it to the "white" category. Even after he was elected president of the republic, Batista was routinely denied membership in Havana's all-white Miramar Yacht Club.

In 1934 some blacks in the city of Trinidad who had been discussing Batista's triumph decided to challenge custom by taking their families for a stroll down the "whites only" section of the central park. Spurred on by old conservatives, a group of white thugs attacked the blacks, hitting them with clubs. The notoriously racist Trinidad erupted in a full-fledged race riot known as "The whitenning of Trinidad." Hundreds of blacks and mulattos were attacked by mobs of whites who swore to "get rid" of all colored people in the city. One of those killed was the noted colored journalist Felix Justo Proveyer. Typically, no convictions resulted from the incident. Batista tolerated this outbreak to avoid angering the white majority.

Batista, who promoted himself from sergeant to generalissimo, opened up the higher echelons of the military to nonwhites. By 1949 the heads of the armed forces and the police were both colored men, as was Batista's chief of staff. However, Cuban whites never stopped resenting the man the white press had labeled *"El Gorila."* Part of Fidel Castro's appeal over Batista may have been Castro's unequivocally white ancestry. Many middle- and upper-class Cubans saw in Fidel Castro the "great white hope" who would deliver Cuba from the uncouth colored rascal who had usurped power for so long.

After Fidel's triumphant entry to Havana on January 1, 1959, some of the rebels with him decided to celebrate at the Hilton, a popular night spot. The white *guerrilleros* were welcomed with open arms, but the colored ones were not permitted to enter. At first Castro did not react, but on March 22, nearly three months after his triumph, he made a major speech on the subject of racism. Castro basically said that the revolution would not tolerate racism. According to an eyewitness, the effect of the speech was dramatic:

> The white bourgeoisie in its entirety, and the white petty bourgeoisie in its majority (including the well-to-do mulattoes), even those who at a time would have given their lives for the revolution, were seized with panic, as if the prime minister of Cuba had announced that an atomic bomb was to fall on the island the following morning. In the rich neighborhoods of Havana, Santa Clara, Camaguey, Santiago, and other cities there was general uproar. The counterrevolution bristled to a man, putting about the rumor that Fidel Castro had invited colored men to invade the aristocratic sanctuaries of the country and dance with any vestal virgin who, up to that moment, had been successfully preserved from the terrible radiation emitted by black skin. This biological menace, this sexual cataclysm threatened not only white flesh, but also religion, the family, private property, and the marvelous indices of the stock market. The whole sinister mythology developed in the days of slavery returned to the surface of men's consciousness. . . . The volcano of Negrophobia was in eruption. . . . Highly

respectable white ladies left the country repeating that, since Fidel Castro's speech, the blacks had become impossible.[15]

Castro himself apparently felt he may have gone too far, for three days later, on national television, he declared that "the revolution is not going to force anyone to dance with anyone else against his will."[16] But one aspect of the Cuban exodus is not often discussed: some of the early exiles did not run away from the red menace of communism but from the black menace—meeting colored people on an equal footing with whites. Significantly, most Cubans settled in what was then racially segregated Miami, where they were more or less accepted as whites. During the American civil rights struggle of the 1960s, Cuban exiles as a group did not support African Americans, just as they have not supported the South African blacks. Cuban exiles and African Americans have yet to find common ground in South Florida, where their relations continue to be very strained.

Although it is no longer publicly practiced, racism continues to be a part of the Cuban ethos. As Booth points out:

> On a personal level, and thus covertly, whites in positions of authority, especially in institutions previously barred to dark-skinned persons, still afford different treatment to individuals of different racial appearance. . . . Black Cubans reported the existence of [such] phenomena to the author in 1969.[17]

Carlos Moore contends that Castro's putative antiracism contains in reality important elements of expediency, condescension, and paternalistic racism.[18] In 1964 Moore found that there were no nonwhite cabinet ministers in Castro's government, which he saw as evidence of de facto continuity between pre- and postrevolutionary patterns of discrimination. (I disagree with Moore slightly in that Castro did have at least one colored man in his cabinet, the durable communist leader Blas Roca, who as a member of the Politburo in Cuba continued until his death in the early 1980s to be the most powerful nonwhite in the island.) Gathering data eight years later in 1972, Booth found that the situation had gotten worse; not only was the cabinet still all white, but the newly created council of ministers, consisting of seven deputy prime ministers, did not include a single nonwhite.[19] Furthermore, Booth found very few interracial couples strolling through the streets of Cuba when he visited in 1969.[20] My own sources in Cuba confirm Booth's findings and stress also that racism has become increasingly overt in the last ten years. Castro's policy of sending mostly blacks to fight in Africa—Angola, Ethiopia, and other areas—has been severely criticized. The practice could be said to have a rationale from a strategic point of view, since black Cubans more easily blend in with Africans; besides, black Cubans, with deep religious and emotional ties to Africa, could ostensibly fight with more enthusiasm for a purportedly black cause. Such rationalizations, however, crumble in the presence of grieving black mothers who wonder why the sons of their white neighbors did not die in the jungles of Angola.

Racism continues to be expressed in Cuba in other more subtle ways; for example, although light *mulatas* traditionally place high in beauty contests like those held during Carnival, no dark-skinned black that I can recall, has been queen of Carnival. It appears as if the worker's paradise has a long way to go before it can claim to be a racial paradise. While it is true that Castro has done away with publicly condoned racism, covert racism and new forms of racial discrimination, such as sending blacks to die in Africa, appear to be on the rise.

Hated by most Cuban exiles, worshiped by many people in Cuba, Castro can be seen as a metaphor for the blend of African and Spanish influences in Cuba. Supposedly a secret practitioner of Santeria, Castro is an amalgam of contradictions, yet the fact that he is aware of the importance Africa has in Cuban history and Cuban reality is undoubtedly a major component in his amazing ability to remain in power against incredible odds. For better or worse, Castro has had an enormous impact on the world, far greater than what one would expect from the head of a small, relatively poor country.

Cuban exiles accuse the Fidelistas of having brought racism to Cuba while the present Cuban regime accuses émigrés of leaving because they could not stand to live in an integrated society. Both positions, while historically wrong, contain a grain of truth. The fact is that racial prejudice, like a lingering boil, has been part of our Cuban heritage longer than anyone cares to admit—and the situation continues on both sides of the Florida straits. One interesting development in Cuban exile communities is that white Cuban santeros are much more obvious than they were in Cuba. Many leading santeros in Miami, including Ernesto Prichardo, Cecilio Perez, and the babalao Carlos Ojeda are white.[21] As one elderly black santera lamented, "lo' blanco' no' jan quitao hasta lo' santo'" (whites have robbed us of everything, even our orishas).

I agree with David Lowenthal's observation, "To be aware of difference is not automatically to discriminate; whereas to be (or profess to be) colour-blind may signal grave anxiety or conceal latent hostility."[22] Lowenthal's statement fits the situation I have described like a glove. Island Cubans, and those in the diaspora as well, sling accusations of racism back and forth, never facing up to their own racial attitudes. Cuban exiles in particular spend undue energy rattling off a list of names of pre-Castro blacks who attained fame and fortune in Cuba. What almost no Cuban wants to remember is that when the most famous black man of his day, Joe Louis, visited Havana in the 1930s, he was denied a room at the Hotel Sevilla.[23]

As even this cursory review demonstrates, Cuban racism exists and has existed for as long as there have been people of African heritage in Cuba. José Marti, whose writings indicate he was a truly unprejudiced man, dreamed of a Cuba where there would not be whites or blacks, only Cubans. Unfortunately, a significant number of Marti's white contemporaries did not share his lofty ideals. Today, Marti's ideas are thought of as the paradigm for Cubans of all races and political creeds. Before Marti's utopic vision can be implemented, however, a realistic assessment of our racial attitudes must be undertaken by Cubans everywhere.

—————————————— NOTES ——————————————

1. David Booth, "Cuba, Color and the Revolution," *Science and Society* XI, no. 2 (Summer 1976), 133.

2. Although some Cubans exhibit Amerindian physical characteristics, the indigenous population of Cuba virtually ceased to exist early in the sixteenth century.

3. Alberto Arredondo, *El negro en Cuba* (Havana: Alfa, 1939), 22.

4. Ibid.

5. Booth, 134.

6. C. Stanley Urban, "El temor a la africanizaçion de Cuba, 1853-55," *Revista Bimestre Cubana* LXXII (Jan-June 1957), 155.

7. Quoted in Robert L. Paquette, *Sugar is Made with Blood* (Middletown: Wesleyan University Press, 1988), 81.

8. For the definitive study of the La Escalera revolt, see Paquette's *Sugar is Made with Blood.*

9. Paquette, 112.

10. Arredondo, 32.

11. Ibid., 33.

12. The Spanish law of *coartacion* allowed slaves to purchase their freedom.

13. Angelina Edreira de Caballero, *Juan Gualberto Gomez* (Havana: R. Mendez, 1954), 118.

14. Booth, 136.

15. Rene Depestre, *Por la revolucion, por la poesia* [For the Revolution and for Poetry] (Havana: Casa las Americas, 1969), 96-97.

16. Ibid.

17. Booth, 158.

18. Carlos Moore, "Le Peuple noir a-t-il sa place dans la revolution Cubaine?" [Black People and Their Place in Cuba's Revolution] *Presence Africaine* 52, 199-208.

19. Booth, 163.

20. Ibid., 165.

21. L. Ernesto Prichardo and Lourdes Prichardo, *Oduduwa Obatala* (Miami: St. Babalu Aye Church of the Lucumi, 1984), 6-7.

22. David Lowenthal, *West Indian Societies* (New York: Oxford University Press, 1972), 1.

23. Arredondo, 72.

GLOSSARY

Aggayú: one of the so-called primal orishas, identified in Cuban Santeria as either the father or older brother of Shangó. He is the lord of mountains and volcanoes.

alafin: title of the king of Oyo.

aleyo: outsider; nonsantero.

asentar: literally, "to seat." In Santeria, it refers to the "seating" of an orisha inside a person's head during the kariocha initiation.

ashé: this dynamic concept has different meanings, among them charisma, luck, mana, spiritual force, and fate.

baba: father.

babalao: Lucumí spelling of the Yoruba *babalawo;* priest of Orula (Ifá); high priests of Santeria.

babalocha: male santero who has sponsored a neophyte.

batá: the three sacred drums used to call down the orishas.

bembé: feast in honor of an orisha, usually involving the playing of batá drums.

botánica: shop where Santeria paraphernalia is sold.

caballo: Spanish word meaning "horse"; used in Santeria to describe the *omo* while he or she is possessed (mounted) by an orisha.

cabiosile: Lucumí spelling of a Yoruba phrase used in Santeria as greeting to Shangó, meaning something like "welcome, lord."

Candonblé: Yoruba religion in Brazil that is similar to Santeria.

collares: emblematic necklaces of the orishas.

despojo: ritual cleansing, usually involving herbs or other plants.

ebbó: sacrifice, offering, or spiritual cleansing.

Eleggua: arguably the most important orisha, the lord of crossroads, the guardian of the gates; also, one of the warrior deities. Eleggua is the first orisha to be propitiated at Santeria rituals.

Eshu: Eleggua's name in Africa; one of the names of Eleggua in Cuba.

guardiero: a talisman or amulet, sometimes made out of a rail spike, used mostly to ward off evil.

guerreros: a mid-level initiation in which the warrior orishas—Eleggua, Ogún, Ochosi, and Osún—are conferred.

Ibeyi: twin sons of Shangó.

iddé: beaded bracelet; usually refers to the yellow and green bracelet conferred by babalaos as protective amulets to be worn on left wrist.

Ifá, ifá: Ifá is a name of the orisha Orula in Africa; ifá is the ceremony in which a babalao is created—"making ifá."

ilé: "house," meaning the house of a priest or priestess and all those who belong to it.

Ile-Ife: holy city of the Yoruba, thought by them to be where Creation began.

Ilé Olorun: the house of God; heaven.

Iroko: sacred tree, in Cuba identified with the silk cotton (kapok) tree.

iyabó: novice; one who has been initiated a santero or santera but has not celebrated the first anniversary of his or her initiation.

iyalocha: female senior santera who has initiated others.

kariocha: also known as "making saint" and *asiento;* the most important ceremony in Santeria, in which the orisha is said to be installed—"seated"—in a person's head. After this ceremony the person is a fully initiated santero or santera.

libreta: Spanish for notebook, referring to the notebooks santeros receive upon initiation that serve as guides for the rest of their lives.

Lucumí: religious, linguistic, cultural, and ethnic identity of the Yoruba people and their descendants in Cuba.

madrina: Spanish for "godmother"; female sponsor.

maferefun: Lucumí for "praised be . . ."

moforibale: the act of prostration in front of senior santeros as a sign of respect.

montada, montado: "mounted," said of a santero or santera when mounted—possessed—by an orisha.

moyumba: litany to the ancestors recited before each Santeria ceremony.

Obatalá: greatest of all orishas.

Obi: in Africa it means "kola nut"; in Santeria it refers to the coconut, its oracle, and its legend.

ocha: an orisha that can be "seated."

oddu: a section of the Ifá oracle.

Ogún: lord of iron, a very strong orisha, one of the warriors.

Olofi: most common name of God Almighty in Santeria; also thought to be the most accessible aspect of God, the other aspects being Olorun and Olodumare.

Olokun: immensely powerful orisha who lives on the bottom of the sea, sometimes thought to be a hermaphrodite. In Santeria, Olokun is thought to be an aspect of Yemayá.

omiero: herbal infusion vital to many Santeria rites.

orisha: the deities or spirits which are the object of active worship in Santeria.

Orula: Orunla, Orunmila; powerful patron of babalaos.

Oshún: orisha of sensuality, owner of rivers.

otán: fundamental stones of Santeria, where the ashé of the orishas is deposited.

padrino: godfather; male sponsor.

santera, santero: one who has undergone kariocha initiation and has finished a one-year novitiate; Santeria priest or priestess. While this term is sometimes used to refer to all participants in Santeria, this is inaccurate.

Shangó: most popular orisha in Santeria; lord of thunder, perfect example of male beauty, and lover of many women, including Oshún, Oyá, and Obba.

Yemayá: orisha of the seven seas, one of the principal orishas in Santeria.

BIBLIOGRAPHY

Angarica, Nicolas V. *Manual del orihate, religion lucumi.* Havana: Private printing, c.1955.

Barnet, Miguel. *Biografia de un cimarron.* Barcelona: Editorial Ariel, 1968.

Bascom, William R. "The Focus of Cuban Santeria." *Southwestern Journal of Anthropology.* Volume 6, no. 1, 1950.

———. *Shango in the New World.* Austin: University of Texas, 1972.

Bastide, Roger. *African Civilisations in the New World.* New York: Harper Torchbooks, 1971.

———. *African Religions of Brazil.* Baltimore: Johns Hopkins University Press, 1978.

Brandon, George Edward. *The Dead Sell Memories: An Anthropological Study of Santeria in New York City.* Ann Arbor: University Microfilms, 1983.

Cabrera, Lydia. *Contes negres de Cuba.* Paris: Miomandre, 1936.

———. *La sociedad secreta abakuá.* Miami: Coleccion del Chichereku, 1970.

———. *La Regla Kimbisa del Santo Cristo del Buen Viaje.* Miami: Coleccion del Chichereku, 1977.

———. *Vocabulario Congo.* Miami: Coleccion del Chichereku, 1984.

———. *El Monte,* 6th ed. Miami: Coleccion del Chichereku, 1986.

Canizares, Raul. "The Epiphany and Cuban Santeria." *Journal of Dharma.* Volume XV, no. 4, October–December 1990.

Castellanos, Isabel Mercedes. *The Use of Language in Afro-Cuban Religion*. Ph.D. dissertation, Washington D.C.: Georgetown University, 1977.

———. Prologue to Lydia Cabrera's *Vocabulario Congo*. Miami: Coleccion del Chichereku, 1984.

Cochran, Tracy. "Among the Believers: Converts to Santeria." *New York Magazine*, October 12, 1987.

Condren, Mary. *The Serpent and the Goddess: Women, Religion and Power in Celtic Ireland*. San Francisco: Harper and Row, 1989.

de Granda, German. *Estudios linguisticos hispanicos, afrohispanicos, y criollos*. Madrid: Gredos, 1977.

Fernandez, Eloise. *The Effect of Spiritism and/or Santeria on Psychiatric Diagnosis of Puerto Ricans in New York City*. Ph.D. dissertation, New York: Adelphi University, 1986.

Ferreira de Camargo, Candido Procopio. *Kardecismo e Umbanda: una interpretaçao sociologica*. Sao Paolo, 1961.

Frischauer, Willi. *The Aga Khans*. London: Bodley, 1970.

García Cortez, Julio. *El santo (la ocha)*. Miami: Ediciones Universal, 1983.

Gleason, Judith. *Santeria: Bronx*. New York: Athaneum, 1975.

Gonzalez-Huget, Lydia. "La casa templo en la regla de ocha." *Etnologia y Folklore*. Volume V, January–June 1968.

González-Wippler, Migene. *Santeria, African Magic in Latin America*. Garden City, New York: Doubleday/Anchor, 1973.

———. *The Santeria Experience*. Englewood Cliffs, New Jersey: Prentice Hall, 1982.

———. *Santeria, the Religion*. New York: Harmony Books, 1989.

Gregory, Steven. *Santeria in New York City: A Study in Cultural Resistance*. Ph.D. dissertation, New York: New School for Social Research, 1986.

Herskovits, Melville J. "African Gods and Catholic Saints in New World Belief." *American Anthropologist New Series*. XXXIX, no. 4, 1937.

———. *Myth of the Negro Past* (1941), 3rd ed. Boston: Beacon Press, 1990.

———. *The New World Negro*. Bloomington: Indiana University Press, 1966.

Howard, Philip Anthony. *Culture, Nationalism, and Liberation: The Afro-Cuban Mutual Aid Societies in the Nineteenth Century*. Ph.D. dissertation, Indiana University Press, 1986.

Kahaner, Larry. *Cults that Kill*. New York: Warner Books, 1988.

Lachatanere, Romulo. *Ioh mio, Yemaya!* Havana: Editorial Caribe, 1938.

———. *Manual de santeria.* Havana: Editorial Caribe, 1942.

Marrero, Manuel. "The Ñáñigo Cult in Ybor City." Paper written for WPA Writers' Project, 1939. In the Special Collections Department, University of South Florida Library, Tampa.

McFadden, Robert. "Ritual Slaughter Halted in Bronx by Police Raid." *New York Times,* May 24, 1980, section 27, p. 1.

Metraux, Alfred. *Voodoo in Haiti.* Paris: Editions Callimard, 1959.

Murphy, Joseph M. *Santeria: An African Religion in America.* Boston: Beacon Press, 1988.

Nogueiras Negrao, Lisias. "Kardecism." *Encyclopaedia of Religion.* New York: Macmillan, 1987.

Ortiz, Fernando. *Los negros brujos* (1st ed. 1906). Miami: Ediciones Universal, 1973.

———. "El origen de los afrocubanos." *Cuba Contemporanea.* Volume IV, no. 11, May–August 1916.

Perez, Cecilio [Oba Ecun]. *Ita, mitologia de la religion yoruba.* Miami: Editorial Sibi, 1986.

Pérez, José "Bangocheíto." *Unpublished Notebook.* Havana: Private Collection, c.1911.

Pérez y Mena, Isidoro Andres. *Speaking with the Dead.* New York: AMS Press, 1991.

Prichardo, L. Ernesto and Lourdes. *Oduduwa Obatala.* Miami: St. Babalu Aye Church of the Lucumi, 1984.

Sandoval, Mercedes Cros. *La religion afrocubana.* Madrid: Playor, 1975.

Simpson, George E. *Black Religions in the New World.* New York: University Press, 1978.

Sosa, Juan J. *La Santeria: A Way of Looking at Reality.* M.A. thesis, Boca Raton, Florida: Florida Atlantic University, 1981.

Thompson, Robert Farris. *Flash of the Spirit.* New York: Vintage Books, 1984.

INDEX